essays

in the face

of uncertainties

essays

in the face

of uncertainties

rob mclennan

Mansfield Press

Library and Archives Canada Cataloguing in Publication

Title: Essays in the face of uncertainties / Rob McLennan.

Names: McLennan, Rob, author.

Identifiers: Canadiana 20220447810 | ISBN 9781771262835 (softcover)

Classification: LCC PS8575.L4586 E87 2022 | DDC C814/.6—dc23

Typesetting and design: Denis De Klerck

Cover photo: Stephen Brockwell

Author Photo: Rose McLennan

The publication of *Essays in the face of uncertainties* has been generously supported by the Canada Council for the Arts and the Ontario Arts Council.

Mansfield Press Inc.

25 Mansfield Avenue, Toronto, Ontario, Canada M6J 2A9

Publisher: Denis De Klerck

www.mansfieldpress.net

for Christine, who was there when it happened

essays in the face of uncertainties : introduction

This suite of pandemic essays, as I've been calling it, exists within those first one hundred days of original lockdown, marking time through moments, anxieties and the elasticity of time itself. What are days, weeks, months? I wanted to document the time, from the swirling, simultaneous anxieties and uncertainties around the constant news-cycle, our small children and the increasing sense of isolation. The shifts, eddys and highlights are interesting to revisit, many of which I'd already forgotten.

It is a strange experience to read through these pieces, nearly two years further down the road from when they were first composed, an array of notes sketched out during and across those first three months of original Coronavirus lockdown. The legion dead, whether directly or indirectly related to the pandemic, and the subsequent onset of Delta and Omicron variants, which keep our household, at least, still home.

There are moments that, once this has all passed, that might become lost, overlooked or simply unknown. While we are moving through the dark, especially with the introduction of multiple layers of vaccine, there is no particular end in sight. I am curious to see who we are once we finally emerge.

May 2022

In times of crisis, we must all decide again and again whom we love.

—Frank O'Hara, *Meditations in an Emergency*

In the beginning of one of his published journals, Jean Cocteau addresses his readers "the unknown friends enlisted by books" and imagines his friends as his "sole excuse for writing them." And reading that sort of validated my sense that though many of my friends may not have accepted my friendship in person (something about our personalities or selves in the way), there was something about their impulse not just to write but to make and share books that encouraged it later. And even his articulation, once shared, gets to be mine as well. I can take on his language and I can be comforted by the support our similarities imply.

—Joshua Beckman, *Three Talks*

•

Nearly two weeks into self-isolation, for the sake of flattening the Covid-19 spread and curve, I spend a full day sorting out the accumulated chaos of my home office. I do this, in part, as a response to this sequence of indistinguishable days. I'd been spinning my wheels. I spend hours gathering and sorting the books on the floor and excess of paper archive. For the first time in more than a couple of years, I'm able to see most of the floor. Able to access the closet. I could mention more, but as Jennifer Moxley writes in *There Are Things We Live Among: Essays on the Object World* (2012): "What you *leave out*, therefore, is a gift. It is as quintessential to the essay as what you put in. To suggest, and then move on."

I shift boxes I'd lost track of, items I hadn't thought of in years. A plastic bag of stones collected from a beach on the East Coast during an eleven-day drive we did when Rose was just shy of a year old. A collection of Ottawa poetry journals from the 1970s. At the back of my closet, I discover the View-Master set I grew up with—a brown plastic box containing dozens of reels and a black stereoscope. I had been seeking an elusive roll of blank paper to entertain the girls, but instead discovered this. For at least half an hour, Aoife sat in our living room couch, quietly absorbed in reel after reel, clicking images at least a decade older than I.

At first I thought it might have been a '60s-era hand-me-down from two cousins, but they say, no, this wasn't theirs. They had one, but not this one.

A quick scan of the internet reveals ours is the View-Master Model E, introduced in 1955, which confirms it belonged to my father. Dates on the reels vary: most are set in the same era, with a few from the later 1960s. "The Coronation of Queen Elizabeth II," for example, copyright 1953, to "Dennis the Menace" and "Wonders of the Deep."

Through these self-isolations, our relationships with the world shift to something far less complex: the binary of outside vs. in. We live in our house, the four of us, with our temperamental cat. Christine and I, along with Aoife, who turns four next month, and Rose, nearly six and a half. Over the past few days, both children have reacted with obvious stress, unable to articulate what we understand full well about being trapped in the house. Most of the time they are their normal, energetic, happy selves, until we see examples of their emotions heightened to unusual levels: Rose becomes more petulant, and Aoife's temper tantrums more frequent, more explosive. We see bursts where they take turns retreating into their bedroom, upset. Seeking alone-time.

What might this mean for how we, as a society, react to potential months of self-isolation? What might social gatherings become once we are able to return to the world? What might schoolyards become? Should I be worried about a generation of children who might emerge slightly muted, slightly more hesitant than they would otherwise have been? All this worry might also be meaningless. The effects are still unknown. We are in the midst of it.

In response to the self-isolations, my friend Stephen Brockwell, the Ottawa poet, has instigated a series of 35 mm portraits of poets through windows. He stands outside, as his subjects remain safe in their houses. He wishes, as he writes me over email, "to document in physical, material ways the Coronavirus." He asks: do we get evening or morning light?

Our front window faces west, and the backyard east. Late March: our yard is still a variety of snow, ice, and water, so I suggest the front window, pushing his opportunities into the afternoon.

Today is warm, the sun out. Soon he stands in our driveway, headset attached to his cellphone, speaking to us in real time. Christine puts him on speakerphone, so we can all hear. A half-second delay between watching and hearing him speak. From within our living room, the girls mug at the front window; Stephen asks us to lean in for framing and proper light.

He catches us all, but within days is forced to abandon the project, given stricter directives around social distancing and remaining home. We all remain home.

Stephen has been engaged with photography the entire twenty-plus years I've known him; he prefers the results of film over digital, for the sake of texture, of depth. While preparing for this project, he told me, he came upon an array of photographs he took of us in 2002, during a reading tour we did of Ireland. A photograph of me, brooding, in front of Yeats's Tower, Thoor Ballylee, the 15th-century Hiberno-Norman tower house in County Galway, once owned and inhabited by the poet William Butler Yeats. "What shall I do with this absurdity, / O heart, O troubled heart—" Yeats wrote, opening the title poem to *The Tower* (1923), about age and experience and hard-won truths. More recently, Ottawa-born American poet Paul Legault reworked his translelation of

Yeats to compose *The Tower* (2020), overwriting Yeats's lines to seek his own discoveries. A transelation, as Erín Moure coined it, from her explorations of creating new work through translating, Pessoaesque, within the language. Legault wrote the first lines of his own title poem: "How will I do being old when I'm old— / having to use this same heart in its place."

What I recall of that day, driving though Galway, was the time Stephen took to set up his tripod, staring down into the top of his camera to frame each shot. As we travelled across Ireland, multiple stops at ruins, churches, and fields where he set up his camera. He had a whole sequence of photographs from that trip. So did I, deciding to take snapshots with my digital camera of Stephen from behind, as he arranged his camera and tripod, although with only Stephen in view. My joke was that it looked from his stance that he wasn't taking photos, but peeing. My photo sequence: Stephen Brockwell, seemingly peeing at important sites all over the country.

What I recall of that day: the tears in his eyes as we pulled up to the tower.

Does peace, in truth, come dropping slow?

●

On March 28, 2020, Ed Nawotka offered this gem in the *Los Angeles Times*, an article I discovered through a social media backlash:

> Looking ahead, only one thing is certain: Writers now have a lot more time on their hands to write. The end of the crisis may find literary agents inundated with fresh manuscripts. The problem is that by then, there may not be enough agents—or booksellers or publishers—left in the business to absorb all the submissions.

A great deal of the response, from what I saw, was from an array of literary writers in my feed, answering in terms of mental capacity: how can anyone get anything done in times like these?

Normal, or at least routine, requires an act of will. If such a thing might even be possible. To admit this conceit betrays my privilege. I have the luxury of remaining home and pondering how we all might survive, both physically and emotionally. My spouse has a good government job and relative security, although a compromised immune system. I never have any money coming in at regular intervals, surviving off, as Toronto writer John Degen suggested some twenty-odd years ago, "hundreds of thirty-dollar cheques." These days my tricklings are certainly far less, although they haven't quite stopped. Not that I can do anything with it, even if it was coming through. Reduced income means the bills stack up; expenses ramp up as we soldier on, bunkered in our three-bedroom lockdown.

In a personal essay for CBC Radio, broadcast March 27, 2020, "These constant prods to do something...are becoming a real irritant," Bill Richardson responded, if indirectly, writing on productivity and self-isolation, and wondering what pressures, say, William Shakespeare might have had to contend with during his own productive isolations.

At least his was a time before social media. A social media, Richardson adds, that keeps reminding us that Shakespeare, by the way, wrote *King Lear* while on lockdown, during an outbreak of bubonic plague. The reminders berate us with their lack of subtlety: just what are you doing with your time, exactly? Richardson writes:

> These reminders, unbidden, popped up in the very early days of the COVID-19 crisis and are still coming thick and fast, on Facebook, on Twitter. And I find them about as interesting and as helpful as hearing from people who, learning that I can invest 45 minutes of sweaty intensity to fret over the placement of a semi-colon, reply by saying that Mel Torme wrote *The Christmas Song* in 15 minutes.

As Puritan minister Thomas White preached outside St. Paul's Cathedral in 1578: "The cause of plagues is sin, and the cause of sin is plays." As an infant during the summer of 1564, Shakespeare had survived an outbreak that decimated a quarter of the population of Stratford-upon-Avon, so he would have known, as a March 2020 article in the *Guardian* suggests, how and why to self-isolate. Although the closing of theatres —meaning a lack of income, social interaction, and performances—would have raised his anxiety, it also prompted the composition of a slew of his greatest works, all exuding their own anxieties: *King Lear, Macbeth, Romeo and Juliet*. Locked within, while still productive.

Part of what I see through social media, in the array of writers, artists, and other creators, is threads that work in both directions, all on the subject of productivity. Some feel pressure to get anything done, unable to work because of a combination of stressful circumstances, from employment, finances, and child care to general anxiety. These are uncertain times, and not everyone employs the same resources or strategies; not everyone faces the same hurdles. Others felt berated for being productive, as though they should be filled with guilt. They felt targeted. How could you.

Or as Lear himself prodded Cordelia, early in the play: "Nothing will come of nothing: speak again."

The children have spent the morning setting up what they're calling their clubhouse, in the centre of our living room, relocating pillows, blankets, and furniture. They remain in the dresses they insisted on sleeping in. Christine makes coffee, far different than mine. I am re-reading Emmanuel Hocquard, from *Crosscut Universe: Writing on Writing from France* (2000), edited and translated by Norma Cole: "The fragment deserves our attention for a moment, if only by virtue of the fact that for some it causes a technical discomfort."

Our six-year-old strolls into my office and asks: "Can I have an apple?"

I was gifted this anthology by Toronto writers Stephen Cain and Sharon Harris, a decade after the book had been published, and I latched on to the prose of Hocquard's poems, and the shapes of the silence he articulated. The catalogue copy for another of his English translations, *The Invention of Glass* (2012), reads:

> This is a *narrative* that tries to explain and to crystalize (the fourth state of water) a situation that has not yet been clarified. Under the guise of memory's particular logic, its play of facets turns to fiction because its sense takes shape only as the series of grammatical phrases unfolds, fusing shadows and blind spots. And yet, like glass, which is a liquid, the *poem* is amorphous. It streams off in all directions, but reflects nothing. What is the meaning of blue? No one needs to interrogate the concept of blue to know what it means.

I am thinking about silence. And space. And the concurrent possibilities and impossibilities of both, especially while home with two small children. I am thinking of silence, and the gift of silence. I listen for the happy laughter, and the complaints, of our two girls, even amid their occasional interruptions, before I leave my desk and attend to their needs. An afternoon of crafts, and the possibility of a walk around the block. Their small boots covered with springtime mud.

Our three-year-old asks: "Can I have some milk?"

Earlier today, Vancouver poet and critic Stephen Collis tweets out a series of small explorations, asking similar questions about distance, silence, and distillations:

> More from work in progress: 1 / I realized then how rarely I thought of other people. The concept was abstract, a part of some other non-monadic world, where multiplicity and the swarm were normal. What did people do with one another?
>
> 2 / What was small talk? What was communicated beneath the words they exchanged—in gesture, in glance or stare, in proximity, in display?

From Hocquard's *A Test of Solitude* (2000), as translated by Rosmarie Waldrop:

> I write that in order to write this.

•

We attempt to make shapes of our uncertainties, even amid the deluge of daily updates. We attempt comparisons. At first, the most prevalent was with the Spanish flu pandemic of 1918, referred to by Richard Gunderman as the "Greatest Pandemic in History." According to his 2018 article on healthline.com: "Between 50 and 100 million people are thought to have died, representing as much as 5 percent of the world's population. Half a billion people were infected." Gunderman goes on to write:

> While few living people can recall the great flu pandemic of 1918, we can continue to learn its lessons, which range from the commonsense value of handwashing and immunizations to the potential of anti-viral drugs. Today we know more about how to isolate and handle large numbers of ill and dying patients, and we can prescribe antibiotics, not available in 1918, to combat secondary bacterial infections. Perhaps the best hope lies in improving nutrition, sanitation and standards of living, which render patients better able to resist the infection.

Comparisons slowly begin to shift into something else: relating to experiences our grandparents and great-grandparents might have felt, during World War II. "Now I finally understand what my grandparents knew," opines American journalist Allison Glock, for CNN, toward the end of March. She writes of informing her daughter, during their self-isolation, of her own grandparents living in cramped quarters, whether baking, gardening, or doing crossword puzzles, having spent their own seemingly endless stretch of time against an uncertain future. She speaks of attempting to survive the big picture by focusing on a sequence of smaller moments:

We will need to find our purpose in the minor things, I tell my daughter. The moments. Moment by moment. We will need to become more like dogs, giddily hopping into the car when we have no idea where it's heading. And in those long, vacant hours, free of clutter and busyness and traditional validation, we will have to learn how to sit with ourselves and discover the glory and meaning in that stillness. Or, at the very least, accept that tomorrow was never promised. In some ways it's no different than it always was, I explain, we just have fewer distractions to hide behind.

Christine, in the kitchen, makes her infamous soup from scratch. Aoife asks me to assist her by carrying their doll carriage down the basement steps. She stuffs a pillow over her doll's body. "So Rose can't see it."
Will we ever be the same? How are we the same?
As part of his response to the crisis, Ottawa artist and historian Andrew King places a toy boat he has built, the *Santa Corona*, down the Rideau River from Manotick, just south of the city. He includes contact details, so any who encounter it can report back the boat's location. He connects remotely to a boat he might easily never see again, and the strangers his boat discovers en route. The *Santa Corona* floats beneath the Manotick bridge, heading north, where it will remain in the river or diverge toward Dow's Lake and the Rideau Canal. Might it get that far?
On Facebook, just now, poet Marilyn Dumont, in Edmonton:

How many small seemingly minor human interactions have now evaporated in the physical world? The tedious LRT ride to campus; the walk through Hub mall, nodding a head & sharing a smile with the occasional shopkeeper or janitor, or passing a student I know; good morning to Leanne at the front desk. Meeting 38 tired, bored, and attentive students T&R for 1.5 hours and the same on Wednesday with 17 students for 3 hours, and (I never thought these strange words would ever come from my live body) committee meetings.

A week into our own isolations, I spend the weekend writing out letters to friends and immediate family. I'd composed more than twenty
letters by Monday morning, all sent out and off in a burst once I did
manage to force myself out for perishables: bread, milk, and fruit. I
mail letters, gather supplies, return home, vigorously wash hands. I've
already seen a shift in the ways in which we interact via social media:
messages sent into the ether are more frequent, more personal, responded to far more often than before. As San Francisco poet Joanne
Kyger wrote to friend and Black Mountain alumni Michael Rumaker,
October 7, 1958: "You owe me a letter but I am feeling unselfish." Is
this how we might connect, instead of retreating deeper into our devices? At our neighbourhood post office, set at the back of the Shoppers
Drug Mart, they've posted a lengthy list of countries that have shut
down their mail services entirely, meaning anything sent their way
would simply remain, for now, in Canada Post storage. I've sent out my
share of email prompts, attempting to touch base with those I wish to
check on, for expediency's sake. Letters take time, as you know. I send
out twenty-three letters and wait. At the end of her letter to Rumaker,
Kyger writes:

> We went to hear May Swenson read at the Poetry Center Sunday
> night and she was Awful. And Jimmy Broughton and George
> Stanley and Ebbe and I were standing during the intermission
> saying that when you hear dreadful poetry like this it makes you
> appreciate how good a woman poet Denise Levertov is and Let's
> all go up to The Place and May Swenson was standing behind
> us all the time hearing every single word. So we had to leave.

●

Early in our isolations, a West Coast poet emails me the text of a letter purporting to be one F. Scott Fitzgerald sent to "Rosemary," as Fitzgerald and his wife were "quarantined in 1920 in the south of France during the Spanish Influenza Outbreak." A century ago on another continent, "Fitzgerald" wrote of what is now achingly familiar: "At this time, it seems very poignant to avoid all public spaces. Even the bars, as I told Hemingway, but to that he punched me in the stomach, to which I asked if he had washed his hands. He hadn't. He is much the denier, that one. Why, he considers the virus to be just influenza. I'm curious of his sources." "Fitzgerald" continues:

> You should see the square, oh, it is terrible. I weep for the damned eventualities this future brings. The long afternoons rolling forward slowly on the ever-slick bottomless highball. Z. says it's no excuse to drink, but I just can't seem to steady my hand. In the distance, from my brooding perch, the shoreline is cloaked in a dull haze where I can discern an unremitting penance that has been heading this way for a long, long while. And yet, amongst the cracked cloudline of an evening's cast, I focus on a single strain of light, calling me forth to believe in a better morrow.

I, of course, took it at face value, before a quick Google search reveals that it's a satire piece written in Fitzgerald's style by Nick Farriella, posted online a week or two prior at *McSweeney's*. I had thought, just a small bit, that it did seem to conveniently tick off all the right boxes: quarantine, handwashing, alcohol. And Hemingway's swaggering, thick-headed machismo. When I mention all of this to Christine, she offers: No, Fitzgerald was far too pretentious to write that. Either way, it does prompt the follow-up: what archive might emerge from these contemporary isolations? Social media feeds, most likely. An endless array of articles and blog entries. Someone tweets, referencing the first Harry Potter movie, how one could see young actress Emma Watson in the background, mouthing the lines of her fellow actors. Does anyone remember which scenes?

I work to not only record the present moment but to fully embrace it. I refuse to lean away from the chaos that these uncertainties bring, but I'm fully aware that, for now, we aren't suffering for food, lodging, employment. Perhaps my perspective is entirely skewed, privileged to such a point that I am unable to even see anything of where we truly are. Hardly suffering, but more of a sheltered sequence of inconveniences. Should I even be speaking?

In *Debths* (2017), Susan Howe: "We have so little time in the distant present."

Walt Whitman's "Give Me the Splendid Silent Sun" from *Leaves of Grass*: "Give me solitude—give me Nature—give me again, / O Nature, your primal sanities!"

U.S. President Donald J. Trump, in his petty, blinkered way, suggests that America can return to work by Easter, which everyone considers unlikely, if not impossible. It prompts comparisons to the character of the mayor in *Jaws* (1976), who insisted the beaches were safe to reopen, also by Easter. In the end, it is never the mayor who gets slapped in the face. Within a week, the president relents and offers the end of April instead. Even that seems optimistic.

One becomes aware of a litany of failures, from social to political. A domino effect. While the president fiddles, America burns. Congresswoman Nancy Pelosi, meanwhile, shakes her head, fumes.

In contrast, our prime minister, Justin Trudeau, emerges from fourteen days in isolation. He was the first world leader to do so, after his wife, Sophie Grégoire Trudeau, tested positive for Covid-19. For two weeks, Sophie lives solo in one part of their home on Sussex Drive, as Justin solo-parents their three children, manages a crisis from his home office, and gives daily press briefings outside their front door. His government, with those daily briefings, quickly projects calm, clarification, resolve. At least one of the briefings is delayed—Justin's youngest child needs a bath. The world is watching.

Even Premier Doug Ford, Ontario's Conservative leader, unexpectedly offers repeated praise to the federal response and to Trudeau himself. Asked about the federal carbon tax, Ford responds: I won't discuss politics until this is over.

Once Sophie Grégoire Trudeau is given the all-clear and allowed to reunite with the family, she relocates with the children to their cottage in rural Quebec, despite the blockades at the provincial border. Prime

Minister Trudeau remains in the official residence, appearing every morning outside his front door for his daily announcements and press conference.

At the same time, Mervyn Horgan, a University of Guelph sociology professor who studies the interaction of strangers in public spaces, notes the corresponding "millions of tiny acts of solidarity," from people out on walks asking how strangers are doing, saying hello on the street, to those reaching out through social media, email, and structures such as food banks. Where are we heading? There is something positive here, and one wonders if such considerations might continue well after the crisis has passed, although crises breed responses that normal life might not necessarily allow.

I attempt to remain positive, in part by remaining productive, although some days I accomplish little or nothing. Should I fold laundry? I offer to read stories to the girls, but only Aoife accepts; Rose is in their bedroom immersed in assembling necklaces for everyone. By dinnertime, she's put together a trio of gift bags.

Christine switches off our daily regimen of CBC Radio 2, concerned the hourly news updates are affecting the girls. She replaces this with an array of CDs, all of which end after less than an hour. The long stretches of silence across our main floor, once unoccupied. Christine and our young ladies, downstairs. I walk through the silence to replenish my coffee.

•

The Unbearable Lightness of Being (1984) might be Milan Kundera's best-known novel, but I have always been partial to *Immortality* (1990). Of course, I can't locate the book in my library. I know I still have it around, but it might live in our storage unit, two-plus kilometres east—a remnant of our two-years'-past basement flood and extensive downstairs reconstruction. I remember first reading *Immortality* when I was twenty-four, and I told myself for some time that the novel had "changed my life," although I can't remember exactly how. That was nearly thirty years ago, after all. Since those days, I've admired Kundera's ability to equally blend elements of the political, philosophical, and intimate, a goalpost I've worked to reach in my own fiction. It's hard to do well, and easier to see when it misses the mark, and Kundera managed to articulate novels from within a period of turbulence, writing of political and social upheaval. I read a debut Canadian novel some twenty years ago that went back and forth between a political thread and a romantic thread, but only one of those threads was compelling, which meant the other lay fallow. At the end of my copy of Kundera's *The Book of Laughter and Forgetting*, he closes an interview conducted by Philip Roth with this:

> I am wary of the words pessimism and optimism. A novel does not assert anything; a novel searches and poses questions. I don't know whether my nation will perish and I don't know which of my characters is right. I invent stories, confront one with another, and by this means I ask questions. The stupidity of people comes from having an answer for everything. The wisdom of the novel comes from having a question for everything. When Don Quixote went out into the world, that world turned into a mystery before his eyes. That is the legacy

of the first European novel to the entire subsequent history of the novel. The novelist teaches the reader to comprehend the world as a question. There is wisdom and tolerance in that attitude. In a world built on sacrosanct certainties the novel is dead. The totalitarian world, whether founded on Marx, Islam, or anything else, is a world of answers rather than questions. There, the novel has no place. In any case, it seems to me that all over the world people nowadays ask, so that the voice of the novel can hardly be heard over the noisy foolishness of human certainties.

While Kundera remains one of the great writers of the Czech Republic's Prague Spring, and one of the finest novelists of the twentieth century, certain elements of his work don't exactly age well. His depictions of women, for one. And yet, he's an example of living, breathing, and writing through the midst of great crisis. Writing as a way of thinking, of documenting. Of processing. How does one write in a crisis?

And crisis is relative, of course. There were those on both sides of Quebec's language debate in the Bill 101 years that Mordecai Richler wrote about in his non-fiction blend of politics and satire, *Oh Canada! Oh Quebec!* (1992), and they saw themselves as the victims of unrelenting crisis. One could also begin to finally ask why there have been water advisories in certain areas, predominantly Aboriginal communities, in Canada at all, let alone some lasting four decades or more? How do we allow such conditions to continue, especially those we have the ability to change? I dread to think of how hard some of these communities could be hit, through this crisis, in part due to their lack of basic necessities, even before any potential access to masks, gloves, and ventilators. How does one write in a crisis?

In the introduction to *Resisting Canada: An Anthology of Poetry* (2019), editor Nyla Matuk writes:

The poems in this book question the triumphalist, nation-building narratives typical of Canada's historiography. As a settler-colony, Canada will only find the road to moral ground once it attempts to understand how and why it sits atop land, cultures, significant landmarks, and memories that do not belong to it, and faces its history of irreversible damage to First Nations Peoples, including its genocidal intent; once the state stops taking for granted that its self-declared presence permits access to unceded lands or entitles it to ignore or transgress the territorial or jurisdictional sovereignty of First Nations.

She continues:

> But colonialism isn't merely a historic phenomenon we can dismiss as irreversible. It's an ongoing set of practices negatively affecting human beings and the environment. The poems in this anthology believe that these practices can be confronted. Such decolonization requires art forms that re-orient a settler society to bear witness to the standpoint of the colonized. Or at least they may offer a gambit in that direction. The point, to borrow a phrase from feminist political theorist bell hooks, is to move the locus of colonized meaning and knowledge from margin to centre. As writer and activist M. NourbeSe Philip tells us, "the power and threat of the artist, poet or writer lies in this ability to create new i-mages, i-mages that speak to the essential being of the people among whom and for whom the artist creates. If allowed free expression, these images succeed in altering the way a society perceives itself and, eventually, its collective consciousness."

I think of Billy-Ray Belcourt's *NDN Coping Mechanisms* (2019), where he writes: "Let us undertake an ethnomusicology of tears. I am after the frequency of NDN grievability. My hunch is that the pitch interrogates itself, like a hymn." I think of Layli Long Soldier's *Whereas* (2017), in which she writes: "But the term American Indian parts our conversation like a hollow bloated / boat that is not ours that neither my friend nor I want to board, knowing it will never take us / anywhere but to rot. If the language of race is ever truly attached to emptiness whatever it is / I feel now has me in the hull, head knees feet curled, I dare say, to fetal position—but better / stated as a form I resort to inside the jaws of a reference."

I might ask how one writes in a crisis, but to many, the very question broadcasts my lack of awareness of the larger world. To some, crisis has been here for hundreds of years. None of this is new.

In Brooklyn, New York, writer and blogger Corrie Hulse posts a blog entry at the end of March 2020, connecting the Spanish flu pandemic with Covid-19. "Apparently," she writes, "during World War I, my great, great uncle Paul was serving in the U.S. Army and was stationed at a hospital in Rouen, France. Among the many family artifacts my cousin has collected over the years were two letters written to Paul in the midst of the 1918 flu pandemic." Hulse's great, great aunt Lucille writes to her great, great uncle Paul, informing him that she, a teacher, has been asked to fill in as a nurse, given that the schools are closed and the hospitals are filling up. From Paul, a medical student, Hulse learns that he, too, has been conscripted for service. With the current number of nearly graduated medical students now being encouraged into service, the parallels are striking. The numbers of retired doctors and nurses returning to service, including the incumbent president of Ireland, Dr. Leo Varadkar. It is, as numerous leaders and medical professionals have offered, "All hands on deck."

The numbers update constantly, from confirmed cases to confirmed deaths. The numbers rise. The number of deaths in the United States, through that country's sheer refusal to deal with the crisis on the federal level, quickly surpasses that of any other country, including China, where the virus is presumed to have originated. The "Chinese Virus," as President Trump calls it. Is anyone still shocked by how blatantly and openly racist he is? A century ago, Spain certainly wasn't pleased about the naming of the Spanish flu. Spain was neutral during the Great War, meaning theirs was one of the few countries that didn't suppress the numbers of their influenza deaths, giving the impression that Spain had an outbreak when other countries did not. Still, some rumours at the time had the Spanish flu originating in multiple countries and corners of the world, including a belief it might have originated deep in the heart of the American Midwest. Should we have called it the Kansas flu?

Quebec numbers rise quickly, due, in part, to more widespread testing. With further testing come further confirmations. This does not mean our Ontario or Ottawa numbers are any better.

There is a text floating around the internet, said to be from a doctor in India, on how so many of the ways we are protecting ourselves from the virus are impossible for much of their population. Washing hands requires running water, and lockdowns require a house large enough and doors to keep closed. Social distancing presumes less of a population density. So many will die, with so many more infected.

Christine says she's thinking of ordering worms for compost after Rose offers it as something we should be doing. Two days later, worms arrive. How does a six-year-old hear of composting? I suspect she might have picked it up from one of her nature shows, most likely *Wild Kratts*. I've never composted, nor did my parents, but my widowed McLennan grandmother certainly did, from her small log house on our same concession road: her compost pile in the far end of her yard, just by the apple tree. Egg shells, coffee grounds, and potato peelings. She kept it to feed her garden.

How much else from those war years is circling back? Rationing and composting. A feeling of dread. Although no actual rationing, per se, but we are asked to avoid hoarding. Reports emerge of worried consumers clearing stores of supplies. Tales of urban dwellers wandering into rural areas and attempting to clear out the shelves.

Articles float through the electronic ether about "moral fatigue," how the body and spirit are simply worn down.

Through all this talk of productivity, there hasn't yet been discussion, at least that I've seen, about how or even if one should approach art through such times. How does one write through a crisis, whether responsibly or even at all? How can anyone create art without it feeling, in some way, useless or extraneous?

One could argue: if art falls apart in the midst of a crisis, what was the point of art in the first place?

In her debut *Open Book* writer-in-residence piece for April 2020, "Writing Communal Poetics in Isolation," Dani Spinosa writes:

Visual poetry is almost inherently a communal genre. Because we are not encoding and decoding meaning in the same way that lyric, narrative, or other more sense-making genres do, visual poetry allows other writers to add, alter, translate, and transform the vispo text. And, I think that's part of what visual poetry does in the time of the coronavirus. It represents a community when we feel distanced. Sometimes it helps. Most of the time, it doesn't. But visual poetry has provided me comfort in my relative isolation when my focus feels too strained and my motivation too low to make sense and meaning out of sentences, paragraphs, narratives.

It is a good question: from where might we find meaning through these lengthy and ongoing isolations, cancellations, and postponements? When might we even see each other again?

Ben Purkert, via Twitter: "There's a part in Virginia Woolf's diary (I'm paraphrasing and don't have the book with me) where she wonders how bombs dropped in London will impact the reception of her book and it reminds me that certain behaviors we writers attribute to social media are in no way new."

When was the last time you went outside? The last time you went out to dinner? The last time you had a drink with a friend? The last time you went to a coffee shop? The last time you went to work? The last time you touched a person outside of your immediate household? When was the last time you saw someone out on the street without flinching?

And some workers are considered "essential" during these times, forced to engage with transit, workspaces, and public spaces, but with a greatly heightened anxiety. My eldest daughter, Kate, still at her kiosk downtown in the Rideau Centre, has begun to have difficulty heading home across the provincial border. When does this end?

In the days leading up to the original shutdowns, we had a meeting for VerseFest, our annual poetry festival: we were twelve days away from our opening night, having spent eight months organizing, but realized what was coming. The vote was unanimous, to shut the festival down and see where we were for something further in the summer, or in the fall. It was a tough decision, but it was in the wind. Within a day, other festivals announced the same. By the following morning, everything scheduled for the following two months was out. The New Orleans Poetry Festival, Vancouver's Room Festival. The Ottawa International Writers Festival.

I had to cancel my birthday party. No—postpone. I had to postpone my birthday party.

So much has changed over the past three weeks.

The late French poet and translator Anne-Marie Albiach, in conversation with Jean Daive (translated by Norma Cole), from *Crosscut Universe: Writing on Writing from France* (2000): "Silence appears. So there is silence."

The days stretch on. By the end of each afternoon, seeing friends' birthdays appear on the top right corner of my Facebook feed. Didn't I already wish them a happy birthday weeks ago? Was that only today? Was that only just this morning?

In "NOT JUST POSTWAR FOCUS, BUT DEEP AND FETID," as part of her half of *Ceci n'est pas Keith / Ceci n'est pas Rosmarie* (2002), Rosmarie Waldrop wrote:

> Things settled down to "normal." The quarrels, the silences. My sister Dorle married and became my refuge. Mother cleared my throat. Every few weeks she moved all the furniture. Father retreated into his astral body, quoting Goethe and working the Rühmkorff pendulum. I barricaded myself behind books.

What is normal? What is silence? Silence is what fills the emptiness, turning an open space into a kind of mass. The difference is whether the mass is one of salve or anxiety. Our girls in their room for far too long without a peep, which makes me wonder what they're doing. When I get up to check, I discover water they've collected from the bathtub stretched out across Aoife's bed, their carpet, and onto the hardwood. They were giving their dolls a bath. A spread of wet towels across the floor. What is silence? By the time I get up, both girls have escaped into the other room. I can hear them.

In what seems a timely article in the *New Criterion*, Montreal poet and critic Carmine Starnino writes on the poet A. M. Klein, who, starting in 1955, retreated into a silence that lasted the remainder of his life:

He stepped down as editor of the weekly newspaper *The Canadian Jewish Chronicle*, quit his law practice, and resigned from the bar. At the same time, Klein took the literary career he had assiduously built and razed it. He gave up writing new poems, abandoned his second novel, and stopped responding to letters. Royalty checks went uncashed. Reprint requests were ignored. When the Royal Society of Canada awarded him a literary medal, he snubbed the ceremony. Most disturbing, Klein effectively ceased speaking. In 1959, two years after his encounter with Edel, he was asked by another visitor if he was working on any new projects. Klein nodded in the direction of his desk, which was bare. So extreme was his self-imposed exile, he skipped his wife's funeral in 1971 and sat shiva by himself, at home. He died the following year, in his sleep, from an apparent heart attack.

Silence is one thing, but how does one keep from retreating until one completely disappears? How does a body or a spirit keep from drowning? By the end of March, several American late-night hosts—Stephen Colbert, Jimmy Fallon, Seth Meyers, James Cordon, John Oliver—have begun to broadcast new episodes, each host secure and solo in the safety of their homes. At first they had taped episodes from empty studios, but that plan quickly faltered into broadcasting a week's worth of repeats. Sometimes attempting normal can't wait until normal resumes on its own. By comparison, Samantha Bee didn't even pause, immediately shifting to taping episodes from the edge of the woods, attended by her husband and their three children: her whole household, conscripted into service. Trevor Noah, who retreated into his apartment, remaining longer than any of his contemporaries, until returning to an entirely reshaped and reimagined studio space, deliberately constructed without live audience.

As Starnino writes of Klein: "He is nearly as well known for the words he never wrote as for the words he did."

•

An article from *Wired* floats across my social media feed, Laurie Penny's "This Is Not the Apocalypse You Were Looking For," dated March 30, 2020:

> There's an important difference between apocalypse and a catastrophe. A catastrophe is total devastation, with nothing left and nothing learned. 'Apocalypse'—especially in the biblical sense—means a time of crisis and change, of hidden truths revealed. A time, quite literally, of revelation. When we talked about the end of every certainty, we were not expecting any revelation. We were not expecting it to be so silly, so sweet, and so sad.

Her article speaks of the unexpected divide between what she calls "apocalypse porn" (films such as *Zombieland, World War Z,* and *I Am Legend,* as well as the wildly popular television series *The Walking Dead*) and the current pandemic, forcing numerous shutdowns, from schools to offices to stores, leaving streets empty of cars, and even of people. But, as she writes, there are no squalls of feral youngsters in roving gangs willing to murder lone survivors over supplies.

> Instead, the world feels larger, not smaller. Right now, with over a third of the world on some sort of lockdown, with the entire world going through some version of the same crisis at once, we are suddenly frantic to touch one another. It seems more important to reconnect with friends. It seems more important than ever to be sweet and silly. We all know someone who's stuck in a house by themselves, trying not to go bonkers. We all know someone who's stuck in a house with someone awful, trying to survive the hotboxing of an already toxic relationship.

And many of us, by now, know someone who's sick.

And yet Netflix numbers announce that one of their most viewed films within the first couple of weeks is *Contagion* (2011), which, according to Christine at least, sets as its foundation the science of approaching and treating the virus that besets the narrative. For my part, I still refuse to watch it.

We are seeing the world change in real time. There are things we did yesterday that we can't do today. There are things we did a week or a month ago that now become unthinkable. Comments emerge on social media about being made nervous watching television or films, flinching when characters hug, or even touch. How could they do such a thing. This must be from last year. As they shake hands.

Rush-hour traffic on Alta Vista Drive: a trickle where there was once a deluge. Where there was once a row of cars some ninety minutes every weekday, from three-thirty onwards.

By Easter weekend, both "#endthelockdown" and "morons" are trending on Twitter, as some, apparently, start getting twitchy. We knew it would come: lower Covid numbers were the results we were waiting for, showing us precisely that social distancing has been working. And yet there's a group of people in Vancouver pushing to return to the world. While the stories of those resisting lockdown are troubling, I've enjoyed how most of the time when something of this sort appears on Twitter, the bulk of the hashtags are from Canadians responding with just how stupid an idea this is. Do you want to get yourself killed? Around the same time, further anti-Trudeau hashtags emerge as well, with similar kinds of smack-downs in response, reminiscent of the meme of Golden Age Batman slapping Robin in mid-sentence. "Trudeau is a fasc—" SLAP. NO.

The outside world becomes imaginary. "In the future," poet Dina Del Bucchia tweets, "when travel exists again." The suggestion of a return to normal travel feels almost too optimistic to consider. Do other cities still exist? Do mountains, or the oceans? Lorine Niedecker, *Lake Superior*: "Inland then / beside the great granite / gneiss and the schists."

We each retreat, in our own ways. But how far, and how deep?

Tweeted out from the Lighthouse Writers Workshop: "Today's writing prompts ask you to push your imagination, constructing a short story or poem using only one-syllable words." Fun, heart, song, burst. Hope. Do these prompts provide meaning, or are they distraction? Are they meant to keep us productive, or from going completely squirrelly as our self-isolation lingers? The Province of Ontario extends the length of the shutdown. We run farther, but the tunnel extends. There is no light. No end.

Christine returns from an outing to our local Costco and regrets every part of it. She reports on a Costco staff member repeatedly yelling at customers to stand closer together while in line. Christine nearly abandoned her cart and fled. Instead, she held on and returned with our car nearly filled to the brim. Re-bagged supplies head to our sunroom for their own isolations, with perishables immediately sanitized and secured in refrigerator or freezer downstairs. An influx of layered, sequestered grocery bags decorates the sunroom, door closed behind. We do this optimistically, as a child barrier. Three days, we've been told, before they are safe to touch and begin to absorb into our pantry, kitchen. Our dinner table.

In *Ongoingness: The End of a Diary* (2015), Sarah Manguso writes:

Living in a dream of the future is considered a character flaw. Living in the past, bathed in nostalgia, is also considered a character flaw. Living in the present moment is hailed as spiritually admirable, but truly ignoring the lessons of history or failing to plan for tomorrow are considered character flaws.

I still needed to record the present moment before I could enter the next one, but I wanted to know how to inhabit time in a way that wasn't a character flaw.

Remember the lessons of the past. Imagine the possibilities of the future. And attend to the present, the only part of time that doesn't require the use of memory.

On the news, I catch reports of refrigerated trucks backed up in some American hospital bays, to house the bodies of those who have succumbed to the pandemic. The morgues are full. There is nowhere else to put them.

Ontario announces an extension of school closures another six weeks, to May 14. Manitoba announces "indefinitely."

Today is the final day of March 2020. Is this lion or lamb?

Through the self-isolations, I've already begun to mark shifts in my mood. Harder to sleep at night, harder to wake the following morning. By the time I do rise, Christine is on the couch on her phone, and both girls on tablets. The muscle along my jawline is taut. I prepare coffee. I put on the kettle for the girls' oatmeal. I turn on some music. Today, Joni Mitchell, from Christine's CD collection. I think it is time the young ladies were introduced to Joni Mitchell. What might be next? Dark thoughts of having to snare and strip small game from the yard. By the end of the day, a stretch of the Ramones, as our young ladies inhale post-dinner ice cream.

There are books one reads and loves, books one never finishes, and books one returns to repeatedly. Once a decade or so I find myself again going through Stan Dragland's *Journeys through Bookland and Other Passages* (1986), a book I first encountered during my twenties. A few years later, I carried it along during a cross-Canada reading tour, re-absorbing essays in VIA Rail coach from Winnipeg to Edmonton, and again, from Edmonton to Vancouver. As one step leads directly and immediately into another, this leads me to other works by Dragland from across multiple of my bookshelves, including his more recent collection of essays, *The Bricoleur & His Sentences* (2014). This leads me further, to this short excerpt from Ottawa writer Elizabeth Hay's novel *Alone in the Classroom* (2011):

A sentence bears the weight of the world. The emotional girl set about baptizing her child. Tess took her dying baby from her bed in the middle of the night and christened him in the presence of her small and sleepy brothers and sisters. Words weigh nothing at all, yet they carry so much on their shoulders over and over and over again.

There is a comfort—and a safety—I've taken in books, for as long as I can remember. When I was young, it was in the books my cousins and mother would read to me, which led to my own history of reading, from Richard Scarry titles to the long list I burned through as part of my grade-school participation in the MS Read-a-Thon. Grade school–era shipments from Scholastic Books, to paperbacks in my maternal grandmother's house: the original *Doctor Doolittle*, or *Cheaper By the Dozen*. The 1960s-era Archie comic books and Illustrated Classics underneath my cousin's bed, or the neighbour down our concession road with his attic space filled with DC Comics. There was my own small collection of comic books, now some 10,000 titles and nearly fifty years deep. And in our wee house, the books that populate this space in the suburbs, a sequence of volumes that multiply at an incredible rate.

What I carry, still, from those superhero comics: How to be resolute and see the big picture. How to get up again. How to, despite all, keep going.

After a week of searching, I finally dig up my copy of Czeslaw Milosz's *Road-side Dog* (1998), a collection of prose poems I remember picking up at a used bookstore along Edmonton's Whyte Avenue in the early to mid '00s, although the receipt inside tells me it was April 5, 2008, exactly twelve years ago this week. My memory had the location correct but not the year. Even Milosz knew the truth, as he writes in "The Past": "The past is inaccurate. Whoever lives long enough knows how much what he had seen with his own eyes becomes overgrown with rumor, legend, a magnifying or belittling hearsay."

I like Milosz's insistence on how memory isn't something internal, but external. Or, as the late Saskatchewan-born poet John Newlove wrote: "The past / *is* a foreign country." What will we remember of the world when the dust begins to settle, and finally clears? Did either of these poems—whether by Milosz and Newlove—even happen the way we might recall? By the time that particular poem found its way into a full-length collection, John had been gone for at least a couple of years.

April 1, 2020, and half the world's population is sequestered in self-isolation, whether recommended or mandatory. In New Jersey, a woman is charged with violating the "stay at home" order, after she is caught allegedly tossing a Molotov cocktail at her boyfriend's house.

Within an hour or two of waking this morning, Rose begins hiding "pretend Easter eggs" throughout the house for her sister to find. Aoife crouches beneath my desk, covering her eyes with her palms. Apparently this is the only safe space away from their game. By the end of the week, they're navigating half a dozen daily costume changes by afternoon, including part of a morning in Christmas pyjamas, lunchtime in fancy dress, and a mid-afternoon of bathing suits and life preservers, swimming across the length and breadth of our living room. The house is a mess, but for now we allow it.

Louise Glück, from "Vita Nova": "Surely spring has been returned to me, this time / not as a lover but a messenger of death, yet / it is still spring, it is still meant tenderly."

The snow melts into ponds, and the sun striates through our front window. Our girls barely notice, having been in the house for too long.

Philadelphia poet Pattie McCarthy posts an image of a box filled with found materials, an archive from a series of walks by one of her three children. There are certain items one can make out through the image, but not all. And certainly not context. McCarthy's attentions through these digital photos are important, and by not including a description of the materials within, what might you imagine such an archive might hold?

The poem "Thanks," by W. S. Merwin, from the Academy of American Poets website, seems to have gained added resonance. It begins: "Listen / with the night falling we are saying thank you." There is something fascinating about the rise in poems being posted on social media during these shut-ins, although I could easily be caught in my own social-media bubble, predominantly following a list of writers, practitioners, and enthusiasts who are seeking salve through literary works. Where else might we turn but to books? The resonance is there,

and one shared with the daily city-wide applause for front-line workers, including medical staff, heard from balconies and windows across
Vancouver, to a similar thank-you in Montreal, as Martha Wainwright
recently led her city in a sing-along of Leonard Cohen's "Hallelujah."
The widespread acknowledgment of those on the front lines has been
gratifying, especially against the growing comprehension of what it is
they're up against, from the numbers of loss, the stories of hospital
overflow, and the frightening shortages of supplies worldwide. Merwin's short piece ends:

> with nobody listening we are saying thank you
> we are saying thank you and waving
> dark though it is

In her "Art of Poetry" interview for the *Paris Review*, Claudia Rankine responds: "The relationship between public engagement and private thought are inseparable for me."

News updates daily projections, new lists of those ill, and new tallies of those who have died. I wash my hands, I wash my hands, I wash my hands. It would be easy enough to move from news update to news update via the various outlets enough that new pandemic information—lockdowns, hospitalization numbers, food shortages, potential deaths, cultural responses—could be continuous throughout the entire day. After a while, all that remains accomplished is an increase in anxiety.

Through all of this, I'm still doing my caregiving weekends for my widower father, who is into the later stages of amyotrophic lateral sclerosis. According to his doctor, this is still possible for me to continue, as long as we aren't out a lot in Ottawa (we aren't) and we're taking necessary handwashing and preparation precautions (we are).

Over the past few days, my father held to his bed with a bowel obstruction. The doctor is working on options, all of which include him remaining at home. Even had we not been mid-pandemic, the lack of exercise his prior hospital visit caused prompts a reluctance to send him away. His muscle loss. A reminder that he wants neither a tracheostomy nor the hospital. His do-not-resuscitate.

Normal life doesn't pause during a pandemic. People still get sick, and people still die, entirely unrelated to the current situation. Even so, every notice ramps us up even further. Did you hear Shirley Douglas died? I liked her. Every name that trends on Twitter prompts an immediate fear. Paul Rudd, oh no. But then: oh, no. Paul Rudd: Happy Birthday!

And now: two friends of mine email separate notices that they've each been handed a cancer diagnosis. Another, her mother in hospital from a stroke, and a further, that his father has died. Life still occurs, a fact that seems rather confusing. Events and work are put on hold; shouldn't these be as well?

Interactions that were once commonplace now involve complications, which in turn offer up an increased stress. Lineups form outside of the few businesses allowed to remain open, so as to maintain distances. Six or eight people in line, roughly six feet between. A pure wash of hand sanitizer. Keep your distance.

I'm fully aware that between my immune-compromised wife and immune-compromised father, the effects could be devastating if I were to catch something. Not to mention Rose, who requires a single puff on her asthma inhaler twice a day. I'm not sure how my eldest daughter is declared essential service, still off to work every day at the Rideau Centre. She directs foot traffic, there to answer your questions about where stores might be, even though the bulk of those stores are now closed. Her anxiety flares every time she leaves her house to head downtown. Mine ramps up just thinking about it.

•

Time begins to dissolve. All time is the same time. Days of the week begin to dismantle, into an unending present.

Is this what is meant by the "distracted middle"?

Robert Kroetsch, opening his *Letters to Salonika* (1983):

Time rewrites every book. We try so to construct a book
that time, rewriting, will make it better.

The world is ending, but
the world does not end.

Like Kroetsch—in the space of his poem, at least—home alone on his fifty-fourth birthday, I remained home on my fiftieth. At the onset of lockdown.

By the first week of April, Rose's teacher has instigated a weekly online group session. Christine and Rose are in the master bedroom on laptop, responding in French. Aoife and I are downstairs.

Remembering that public-service campaign from the 1980s: Do you know where your children are?

Allana Harkins, co-producer and correspondent for *Full Frontal with Samantha Bee*, speaks in an interview of the benefits of these lockdowns to booking guests: everybody is home. There isn't anyone who says, "Oh I can't, I'm flying that day." Everybody is home. I ask again: do you know where your children are?

They're at home. We're at home. Everybody is home.

If you seek information online on *Love in the Time of Cholera,* you quickly discover the infamous novel by Colombian Nobel Prize winner Gabriel García Márquez was first published in the original Spanish in 1985 as *El amor en los tiempos del cólera,* and in English translation in 1988, with an English-language movie adaptation released in 2007. Set during the half-century period between 1880 and 1930, the main prompt of the book is that lovesickness is an actual illness, one the novelist compares to cholera; one suffers from love in the same way one might suffer from any ailment: "He was still too young to know that the heart's memory eliminates the bad and magnifies the good, and that thanks to this artifice we manage to endure the burden of the past."

The comparisons with any potential *Love in the Time of Covid-19* novels don't entirely fit, as Márquez composed his metaphor of illness against a distance of some decades after an actual cholera pandemic. Wikipedia notes: "Seven cholera pandemics have occurred in the past 200 years," citing them as 1817–24, 1829–37, 1846–60, 1863–75, 1881–96, 1899–1923, and 1961–75. The bulk of those would have been outside the period during which Márquez composed his novel, although certain elements of one or more may have been within his or his family's memory. Wikipedia, as well, presents the added caveat that numerous cholera outbreaks have also been recorded, "such as a 1991–1994 outbreak in South America and, more recently, the 2016–20 Yemen cholera outbreak."

I've a friend who complains that none of us should be posting our Covid-19 poems or writing those *Love in the Time of Covid-19* novels, although I'm sure most of those attempting theirs have never actually read the source text. It's not only that he doesn't want to see them, but that he doesn't think we should be writing them. He might be right—perspective from the outside is very different from the inside—but the qualities of the inside can't be seen in the same detail once we're done.

In "Art During the Time of Coronavirus," posted online at *Maclean's* on March 24, 2020, Montreal writer Heather O'Neill observes: "Throughout history, art has continued to be created and consumed during times of plagues and global health crises. So art will be created now. Which begs the questions: What sort of art has been created during pandemics? And what purpose does art serve during them?" She offers, instead, *The Decameron* and a variety of plays by William Shakespeare, as well as the comfort she took from the film *Contagion*. "There is a famous photograph by artist David Wojnarowicz," she writes, "who was diagnosed HIV positive in 1987, where his mouth is sewn together with thick thread, attesting to the silencing he was facing, that puts me in mind of St. Sebastien." She writes of art as both comfort and spotlight, as both process and document, being an essential aspect of how a culture processes the difficulties of dark times, refusing to shy away from what needs to be both acknowledged and understood.

> In whatever form it takes, art will be created during plagues. There will be more of a demand for it from people, from those who want to be amused, those who want to be consoled, those who are looking for a community, and those who want to be able to be heard. These periods of hardship indelibly mark art. It changes its subject matter, but more importantly, it changes the very structure and possibilities of art. And all art that follows contains the echoes and scars of all we have been through.

With uncertainty comes fear. It can't be helped. Most of us lean either into the far end of barely functioning or into panic mode. Frontline workers run their bodies down—tales from the hospitals and other services at the forefront of a global pandemic.

In her essay "Eco-logic in Writing," the late American poet Leslie Scalapino wrote: "Seeing at the moment of, or at the time of, writing, what difference does one's living make? What difference does one's living make in '*that*' space, and in relation to spaces all existing at once there?"

●

In "Finding Words for This Pandemic in Inupiaq" for the *Yale Review*'s "Pandemic Files" series, Inupiaq American poet Joan Naviyuk Kane writes:

> Our phone calls with my mother punctuate the days now. My sons record words in our dialect and learn to make sentences. They ask her questions. We don't speak of the future, and I don't want to ask too much about her mother—orphaned in the 1918 flu pandemic. My grandmother's parents and three siblings were all killed by the flu at Qawairaq (Mary's Igloo) on the Seward Peninsula, where, according to ethnohistorians, the mortality rate was 54 percent. I don't ask about the baby boy who died, according to church records, at the orphanage where my grandmother and her two sisters were raised through early childhood.

How does one reconcile the present—setting aside the future for now—with such an unresolved past? Old wounds and losses are brought to light, ones that might never fully heal, but instead drift out of memory as those who remember also fade away. Through a handful of essays over the past few years, Kane has emerged as one of my favourite writers of creative non-fiction. She explores history, culture, displacement, and poetry in a remarkable series of essays that ripple outward from the core of her own centre as Inupiaq, and her mother's traditional home of King Island, Alaska. As she discusses in her stunning four-essay chapbook *A Few Lines in the Manifest* (2018), King Island is an island in the Bering Sea abandoned in the mid-1900s due to forced relocation via the Bureau of Indian Affairs.

I once spoke with a Danish journalist about the relationship between language and survival, how my sons know well the Inupiaq words for airplane (*tinmuzun*), pencil (*aglaun*), tomorrow (*ublaakun*), but how they did not know many words for traditional subsistence food or its harvest, because our lives did not include hunting. Their father is not Inupiaq. He cannot legally harvest a single seal (*niqsaq*), bearded seal (*ugruk*), or walrus (*aiviq*).

She offers her thoughts on the future through her two sons, and what they might hope to inherit, a concern that continues through this new piece, as Kane works through, with, and against a sequence of crises, of which this is both only the most recent and a particular kind of culmination, writing of self-isolation with her two children:

I consider the stretch ahead: how much closer we might grow, how clear our boundaries might become. We're fortunate to weather this here. We read. I write much less than I hope to. I wonder when things will change. I wonder if things have ever stopped changing for my family—for my mother, my sons. For my community. I think about our changing, living language, too. What do I convey to my children?

There are shoes dumped in our living room. Why are so many of our children's shoes dumped in our living room? Our young ladies have, of course, already fled.

Someone offers Carina Wolff's "7 Signs You're Spending Too Much Time Inside & It's Affecting Your Health," originally posted February 13, 2018. Wolff's list comprises "Moodiness," "Anxiety & Restlessness," "Sleep Troubles," "Poor Immune System," "Bone & Muscle Weakness," "Changes in Appetite," and "Fatigue." Articles such as these feel slightly outdated, attempting to gift what most of us have already discovered.

I don't even know what I'm reading. I'm poking through Denver poet Julie Carr's *Someone Shot My Book* (2018), rereading essays even as I compose her a letter, which might not make the mail for another week or two. "Since threat is everywhere," she writes in the opening essay, a piece that provides the book its title, "and most of all at home, there is no moment that one should not be on 'high alert.'" As I read her piece on American gun violence, there is the realization that the global pandemic and subsequent lockdown have prompted—as *Washington Post* reporter Robert Klemko tweets—the first March since 2002 without a school shooting in the United States. What are we to do with this? This fact provides both an immediate relief and an intense sadness. What am I to do with this as a writer, but also the father of three, two of whom are still in grade school? In "Rosmarie Waldrop in Conversation with Ben Lerner" from Rosemarie and Keith Waldrop's *Keeping / the window open: Interviews, statements, alarms, excursions* (2019), Rosmarie Waldrop says:

I am afraid, as Wittgenstein said of philosophy, that poetry leaves everything as it is. On the other hand I believe that poets are the maintenance crew of language, that it is the social function of poetry to keep language (and, through it, thinking) alive and in good working order. But whatever effect poetry has in this way is very slow and long-range, not useful as a political tool. In short: unresolved contradiction.

"We will meet, again," Queen Elizabeth II offers, to close her April 5 address, only her fourth or fifth non-Christmas public message over her ninety-four years. It was a striking broadcast, one that held deep, emotional resonance, punctuated by that final line. Stay home, stay resolute. We have faced challenges before, however different the circumstances. We will get through this. She releases a further, shorter broadcast for Easter a week later, repeating similar prompts.

Vera Lynn's 1939 hit, "We'll Meet Again," was the most well-known song of World War II—Pink Floyd included her name as part of *The Wall* (1979) to throw back to that time and that sense of loss of soldiers sent to war, many of whom never returned. The song was one of longing, but also one of enduring hope. We will meet, again.

As well, I was this many years old when I discovered that Vera Lynn, born March 20, 1917, was actually still alive. Did you know she was still alive? Living in Sussex, South East England, next door to her daughter.

●

Through a CBC News Network piece, I catch an excerpt of a televised Zoom interview with *Schitt$ Creek* co-creator and co-just-about-everything-else, Dan Levy. He offers that these self-isolations make him appreciate the time he has been able to spend with his friends and his family, even virtually. It makes him more attentive. Will these days make us more aware of each other? I would think the immediate result would be certainly, yes. Attentions on isolations, climate, capitalism. How much we purchase, use and throw away. I think of my McLennan grandmother, a former one-room-schoolhouse teacher and World War II–era housewife and newlywed who recycled materials and composted through to the end of her life. I think of her cupboard filled with washed and stored Styrofoam meat packaging, occasionally pulled out for me to utilize as craft supplies. Might we be forced to become more attuned to discarded packaging for our own childrens' crafts? Where might we be in six months, or six years?

I set aside empty cartons from Rose's chocolate milk, and cardboard tubes from toilet and paper towel rolls. We set aside boxes.

What adds an edge to this whole experience is how powerless it makes so many feel. How impossibly small one person's activity or engagement is on the larger scale. The difference lies, I suppose, in how we choose to respond: yelling at shopkeepers or bus drivers or the police won't make the pandemic go away or keep us safe. Neither will storming the gates. How we desperately need to trust that those working the science, those working the medical fields, and those working the government systems will do the right thing, in the right ways, at the right time. And how easily so much of this could go terribly wrong. And how much of it might even not make a damned bit of difference.

And through it all, many writers on my Twitter feed reacting to the award notifications for the annual Guggenheim fellowships, from the handful of frustrated tweets to ones of joyous, stunned shock. For both, earnest reactions of condolence or congratulation, depending. The world is not done with us yet. The world continues.

In the midst of our isolations, we're already deep into the third season of *Schitt\$ Creek* via Netflix, binge-watching since all of this began, well behind this month's sixth-season series finale. A show about a formerly wealthy family who has lost everything, a family suddenly without resources, holed up together in a small space, slowly and eventually discovering new things about themselves and each other. The mind seeks out patterns; am I seeing parallels everywhere I turn? American poet Heather Christle offers, through *The Crying Book* (2019):

> Perhaps it would be truest to allow two stories to correspond briefly, to align themselves into one moment as they travel on their separate orbits, to know that the instant of recognition of sameness must not last. Now the moon is a sorrowful face, now "a rock with blue scrapes." The lines are neither parallel nor perpendicular, but two arcs that momentarily intersect before traveling on. A meeting need not be an end.

An article floats by, through Twitter, titled "Writing in Suspended Time," but the screen self-refreshes and I lose it. I can't find it again. I have no idea what it might have said.

•

On April 7, 2020, the Atlantic posts an article by conservative staff writer David Frum, "This Is Trump's Fault":

> Trump now fancies himself a "wartime president." How is his war going? By the end of March, the coronavirus had killed more Americans than the 9/11 attacks. By the first weekend in April, the virus had killed more Americans than any single battle of the Civil War. By Easter, it may have killed more Americans than the Korean War. On the present trajectory, it will kill, by late April, more Americans than Vietnam. Having earlier promised that casualties could be held near zero, Trump now claims he will have done a "very good job" if the toll is held below 200,000 dead.
>
> The United States is on trajectory to suffer more sickness, more dying, and more economic harm from this virus than any other comparably developed country.

The numbers are terrifying. The refusal to properly respond by the White House and the administration's endless failures are terrifying. Yes, there are those on the front lines working as hard as possible to save lives. New York governor Cuomo, for example, even as his own brother—a CNN anchor—is in self-isolation, having developed symptoms of Covid-19. Within days, #TrumpBurialPits begins to trend on Twitter, with the discovery that many of the bodies of New York victims of the virus have begun to be buried in mass graves on Hart Island. Pine boxes arrive by the truckload, with news photos spreading out across social media.

New York's Hart Island has been used for more than a century to bury the unclaimed dead, or those with family unable to afford a funeral.

With possibly a million burials to date, to that list we add these. On April 10 alone, according to news reports, another forty pine boxes. The same day, the *Guardian* reports on the two sides of New York, as those who are dying are predominantly low-income people of colour in increasingly overloaded hospitals; most of these deaths emerge from the front lines, whether bus drivers or hospital support, working in lower-income jobs that keep the machinery of the city going, while those who can afford to stay home remain there and order their food online, thanks in no small part to a population that appears to be seen as expendable, sent off to work with little or no protection:

> Day by day, the statistics tell their own grim story. On Tuesday, the New York City death toll overtook that of 9/11 and now stands at 3,602 (2,753 died in the city in the 2001 terrorist attacks). On Wednesday, it was announced that New York had suffered its highest number of fatalities in a 24-hour period—806 lives snuffed out in just one day.

An American poet mentions to me in an email that none of her friends are writing, which I find difficult to hear. Even to me, my hastily typed response displays a far more positive emotional state than I would have thought:

> Sad to hear your friends aren't writing; isn't this what writing is, and should be? Both a shelter from the storm, and a way to walk fully out into it, protected; a way for the storm to make sense, and lose much of its power; for us to describe the storm, for all else that sat through it; to see it in the way that it was, and what happens next, after the storm finally passes.

Perhaps, here, I've answered my own question. How does one write in a crisis?

•

It's curious to see, through my father's television, the array of commercials directly responding to the pandemic, from the thank-yous to the empty streets that, once this is over and they can wake, will require a great deal of catching up. Let the roads sleep, Mazda offers.

I don't even want to think about Krakatoa, how it begins to erupt.

The BBC reports on the emergence of the "Belper Moo," as the population of the town of Belper, Derbyshire, daily and in unison, "gather on doorsteps and lean out of bedroom windows for a two-minute cattle chorus." Derbyshire sits in the East Midlands of England, with Manchester and Nottingham on either side, in case you weren't aware. I had to look it up as well.

The "Belper Moo" was originated by one of the village locals, Jasper Ward, who expected it to end after a few days, including possible ridicule, and yet he's done this daily at 18:30 for weeks, with a group that has grown to include hundreds of others. "I seem to have unearthed a madness that has only been complemented by this lockdown," he said. "It's a pretty grim time, so if we can cast a little bit of silliness into the day, that's great."

Also, due to the current pandemic, it is reported, the scheduled *Friends* reunion is unable to film. In response, someone tweets: *Thank you, Covid-19.*

"Writing is always and forever a social practice," Montreal poet and critic Erín Moure writes, to open one of the essays in *my beloved wager: Essays from a Writing Practice* (2009). "The varying discourses in a society either shore it up or challenge it. And discourse isn't something we can walk away from when we set down our pen." I've been rereading Moure as a particular kind of salve against the squirrelliness of lockdown, nearly a month in. It swells inside me like a balloon. Her work is striking for the way she interplays a variety of threads, languages and conversations, as well as the music of her language, and I've been moving back and forth between the signed copy I have on my shelf and Christine's signed copy. When two writers merge their libraries, what might you expect to happen? We had boxes' worth of doubles, deciding to remove only unsigned duplicates as extraneous.

Someone points out that today, April 13, 2020, is actually the birthday of Samuel Beckett, born this day in Dublin in 1906. "Why this farce, day after day?"

We might be Easter Monday, but the day Beckett was born was Good Friday. At least one difference between the days. And what are days anymore?

And in three days, our Aoife, my third and youngest child, turns four. Another birthday in lockdown. Christine suggests that hers, in June, will be our third consecutive lockdown birthday. Might we be open by November, for Rose? We really have no idea.

How does one write in a pandemic? Over the weekend caregiving my father, I compose another twenty letters to a variety of friends. I hope to get them out by the end of the week. In today's mail, a copy of Lisa Fishman's latest poetry collection, *Mad World, Mad Kings, Mad Composition* (2020). At least we still have the mail, declared an "essential service," although one never knows how long that might last. A couple of weeks back, Fishman responded to an email I sent her that she was in a "rented R.V. having driven 2,000 miles one-way to rescue my mother with a lung/respiratory condition to get her from Arizona to Michigan." Wherever she is now, I hope they're both safe. The first lines of her new collection offer:

> Truth-telling is possible, thought Laura Riding, so the poem does not need to happen. That is, poetry should not exist. Rather, language should speak truth in all ways. Not in a separate realm, a special form, called poetry. Poetry existing as a separate category prevents language from speaking truth outside of poetry. Her decision therefore: No more poems. Write a dictionary. Where is this dictionary? Florida?

Responding to my follow-up email from earlier today, Fishman informs me that everyone in her space is safe, and on lockdown, with her mother and her mother's husband safely into Michigan, although "straight into the virus 'hotspot' of metro-Detroit." Through the distances, all our conversations are immediately shaped over safety, health. How are you, really? The nature of pandemic forcing a shift in how we approach each other, even through the most casual interactions. Everything, as I've said, becomes heightened. Further in Moure's essay "Breaking Boundaries: Writing as Social Practice, or Attentiveness":

> Discourse, then, has to be questioned, turned over, or it shores up what is, for me, an oppression and silencing of others. It shores up my own silencing! It is a tacit agreement with the status quo. Every word we write can do this, fall into this tendency, or it can be attentive and can subvert it, reveal its seams, push it sideways. This oppressive tendency, remember, is not solely an outside pressure imposed upon us by the world of ideology and consent: it's inside. We carry it within us. You can't easily see a structure from inside. Yet focusing on the language can help us find its boundaries, rub up against them, and see what changes, what enters.

On *Late Night with Seth Meyers*, actor and comedian Jim Gaffigan speaks to the effect this pandemic and lockdown are sure to have on his children: the particular kind of fear his teenagers are living through, one he says his generation didn't encounter: "This is going to shape them."

Our two girls, once again, pad the upstairs hallway with cushions, change into their bathing suits. They spend the morning swimming laps from bedrooms to living room, jumping from the mouth of my home office into their imaginary pool. A yoga mat in the kitchen, so they can take turns sunbathing. What might be their takeaway from this? What might be the long-term effects on them? Even in lockdown, both Gaffigan and Meyers admit their appreciation of the family time the pandemic allows. Our two girls taking turns leaping, shrieking, past the doorway into impossible depths made suddenly, beautifully possible.

In her "Rachel Rose's Writing Space" posted on *The New Quarterly*'s web page, Vancouver poet Rachel Rose writes:

Slowly you cut off the physical. Each day more curtailed than the one before it. You learn to love people only through the mediation of devices. Your nephew reaches for your face through the screen.

You will become the generation known for saying hello by waving while backing away slowly.

In a piece for the University of Chicago Press's *Chicago Blog*, Charles Bernstein offers his take on current politics, National Poetry Month, and the effects of pandemic and self-isolations in "Poetry Month Will Come a Little Late This Year," writing: "The temporary loss of our physical commons is devastating. But the commons needed now is imaginary not territorial." What else can be said?

In a clip for *Entertainment Tonight*, Jann Arden suggests that her years of working from home have prepared her for this. She is used to working quietly, and in seclusion. Wasn't there an idea floating around a few years ago of Jann Arden and Biff Naked co-hosting a daytime television show? There's an opportunity there, somewhere.

In her piece "Think This Pandemic Is Bad? We Have Another Crisis Coming: Addressing Climate Change Is a Big-Enough Idea to Revive the Economy" for the *New York Times*, posted April 15, 2020, Rhiana Gunn-Wright writes:

> If history is any indication, rebounding from an economic disruption this large requires an equally large spike in demand and production. Outside of war, climate change is the only issue large enough to provide such a spike. Now is the time to create policies that provide immediate relief to communities, such as federal assistance to transition homes and businesses to renewable energy; give "green" fiscal aid to states; and fuel economic recovery with the creation of federally funded green jobs. But none of this can happen so long as our leaders keep convincing themselves that the greatest country in the world cannot walk and chew gum at the same time.
>
> A climate-focused economic recovery—much less a coronavirus response that acknowledges the climate crisis—could require a new Congress and a new president, a tall order in an America this divided. But maybe it is time to stop acting as though politics is a force of nature when we are facing *actual* and deadly forces of nature. It's past time to elect leaders who are fit to handle the crises we face, instead of hoping for problems small enough to fit the leaders we have.

My eldest daughter barely makes it home across the provincial border, recently closed by the Quebec government for "non-essential travel," despite her paperwork that declares her an "essential" worker. She lives in Aylmer, Quebec, but works in downtown Ottawa. She's told, in no uncertain terms, that she won't be able to return to Ontario. She's verbally assaulted by police sans masks along the interprovincial bridge and knows full well that some of their own have already tested positive. At least she's home. At least she doesn't have to go back out.

The *Ottawa Citizen* posts an obituary for Otto Graser, who died April 6 "due to COVID19-related illness." During the 1990s, when he ran the bookstore Arlington Books, he produced some letterpress poetry broadsides and small poetry chapbooks, including one each of mine. Described as "a founding father of the Ottawa Press Gang," he filled notebooks with doodles he used in his printing and artwork, most of which, he said, were made during work meetings, from his time in the federal civil service.

He ran an antiquarian bookstore as a semi-retirement project, doodling and tinkering at his desk at his leisure, in between customers.

We've been sequestered now a full month, since the day I turned fifty. My entire fifties-to-date on lockdown. The beard I'd developed by March—the result of an extended period of distraction—shaved down weeks ago, to highlight mutton chops. My clean chin and neck, with side-brushes. I had long considered side chops, but now seemed as good an opportunity. In my mind, I was aiming for a nineteenth-century "Father of Confederation" look; instead, I seem to channel Lemmy from Motörhead. Or some American Civil War–era general. For now, it suits me. For now, it amuses, in part because there isn't anyone around to see it, apart from Christine and the girls, none of whom really pay that much attention.

A friend of ours mentions in an email that she and her spouse both tested positive for Covid-19. It knocked out their energy for a couple of weeks, she said, but they're coming through the other side. Fortunately, as well, their small children tested negative.

As part of his own essay for the *Yale Review*'s "Pandemic Files" series, "The White String: Dreams of Connection in Quarantine," American poet Brandon Shimoda writes:

> A menacing silence has befallen the world. I imagine that the silence, and its menace, is much louder—maybe even extremely loud—in places that are not the desert, that are far from, or inversions of, the desert. But in the desert the silence is faithful. By faithful, I mean also: watching. As we walk through the neighborhood, people appear—young people, old people, people on bicycles, people with dogs—but disappear just as quickly, as if they had slipped through a sleeve in the more general mirage of sociality in the age of COVID-19. Although it feels more as if the people are the mirage, from which I cannot discount my family or myself. And it feels as if the world—certainly the wide and languid streets of Tucson—is the empty room beneath the grid of white string, which still, in our absence, connects us all, maybe even more intensely.

As of today, there are no posted updates on artist Andrew King's *Santa Corona*. Is it trapped in the weeds by the Rideau River? There, too, a silence, shaped around an absence.

Has it been only a month? Perhaps we've always been here. Aoife wakes up this morning a four-year-old. Rose is excited. She helps Aoife open her presents, seemingly more eager about today than her sister is. Torn wrapping paper scatters across hardwood. My sister and her family gift Aoife a pan flute, which the girls share for now, fighting only occasionally.

Mid-morning, a plumber arrives to assist with a clog in our bathtub drain. He wears a face mask. We send the children downstairs.

The whole past week, I've been preparing an expansive mailing of new publications, including the new issue of my quarterly poetry journal, *Touch the Donkey*. Fortunately, most of the issue was physically printed weeks prior to lockdown, allowing me to simply fold and staple at my leisure, and announce at my regular schedule. I still had to fashion makeshift covers from black paper and printed sticker sheets I had in my paper supply, which made for a perfect pandemic lockdown effect. I'm aiming for a single trip to the post office, with not another for at least a week, possibly two. All those letters from the past weekend, and other scatterings. I am eager, but nervous.

In our sunroom, the tulips burst from the row of bulbs Christine and the girls have placed in glass containers on the window ledge. They check on it daily.

I've a friend in South Brooklyn who says she remains unaffected for now, teaching all her classes online, but she has known some who have died.

On its website, *Lapham's Quarterly* has begun a new series: "In the weeks ahead, as the world continues to reckon with and respond to the COVID-19 pandemic, we will feature voices from the past who told stories that rhyme with the one unfolding before us—stories dealing with quarantine, unfathomable deaths, isolation, dread, and attempts to find community when the rest of the world feels far away." So far, they've featured entries by Heinrich Heine, John Keats, George Eliot, Willa Cather, Lucretius, Thomas Mann, and Jack London, as well as a sequence of diary entries by Samuel Pepys from 1665, when it was "likely that nearly a hundred thousand people—a quarter of London—died during the Great Plague." His entry for August 31, 1665, includes:

> Up and, after putting several things in order to my removal, to Woolwich; the plague having a great increase this week, beyond all expectation of almost 2,000.
>
> Thus this month ends with great sadness upon the public, through the greatness of the plague everywhere through the kingdom almost. Everyday sadder and sadder news of its increase. In the City died this week 7,496, and of them 6,102 of the plague. But it is feared that the true number of the dead this week is near 10,000; partly from the poor that cannot be taken notice of, through the greatness of the number, and partly from the Quakers and others that will not have any bell ring for them.

A month into lockdown, projections suggest we could be in the midst of this for another eighteen months; until a proper vaccine is discovered, constructed, and distributed. A month in, and we're already flailing and failing our attempts at home school, missing at least one of Rose's scheduled classroom Zoom sessions. The girls build cities with blocks in our basement, and work on their game in the yard with a plastic bat and an array of plastic softballs.

I move through further pieces by Rosemarie Waldrop, this time from *Blindsight* (2003). Her work is never far from reach. At least three of her books at any given time rest at arm's length.

> Exchanges public life for uncertainty, reflection, apprenticeship of death. Reads everything, quotes everybody, but does not look in the mirror held up by woman. We Bordelais. Urine full of painful gravel. Without embarrassment, the animal

body. Objectivity, a wish fulfilled only in dreams. Soon after, the kidney disappears from literature.

As I spend my days frantically working through text, Christine works a craft with our girls, at our kitchen peninsula. It would be an island, but it is, after all, attached to the counter, the wall. Through hiding out, still, in my office, I wonder: just what of theirs might I be missing out on?

One of the final poems in CAConrad's *The Book of Frank* (2009) reads:

Frank is a
young boy
asleep in
ancient
Tibet

what you
thought was
your life is
really his
dream

he may
wake at any
moment

There was something in Neil Gaiman's expansive *The Sandman* that spoke in similar directions: the city, and the dream of the city. What might happen to us if our city wakes? Anne Carson once wrote an entire essay on sleep, presented to the League of Canadian Poets as a lecture during our 2004 AGM, held that year at a hotel in downtown Montreal. "This lecture will last fifty-eight minutes," she told us, according to my notes from the time. There were dozens of poets from across Canada around large, circular tables in the hotel's banquet hall, shoved close as Anne Carson spoke to us on sleep. Would to have remained awake through the entire lecture have been compliment or insult? To have drifted away? The piece was subsequently collected in her *Decreation* (2005) as "EVERY EXIT IS AN ENTRANCE (A Praise of Sleep)," where Carson wrote:

> The dream of the green living room was my first experience of such strangeness and I find it as uncanny today as I did when I was three. But there was no concept of madness or dementia available to me at that time. So, as far as I can recall, I explained the dream to myself by saying that I had caught the living room sleeping.

Carson suggests that rooms, that houses, might be able to sleep. Her title also suggests you can always leave the way you came in. Remember that.

Gaiman's lead character in *The Sandman* is Morpheus, Dream-Lord of the Endless, so it would be an understatement to say that sleep is an important element of the series. Dreams might be a different reality than the waking world, but that doesn't make them less real. One of the most striking moments appears early on in the series, as those in the waking world, asleep due to the "sleeping sickness," are freed from their bonds. Some had been asleep for days, or even weeks, and others for decades. They were asleep and, as suddenly, they were not. Awake at the flick of a switch, as they say. "And then she woke up."

It begins to feel as though we've been in the house long enough that individual days no longer exist. The edges of each morning shimmer, as each evening falls in on itself. The children have always been. We have always been. We have always been here.

Days alternate snow squalls and sun, each one overtaking the other.

Newly announced guidelines by the City of Ottawa recommend that, while the girls and I might be able to go out for walks, Christine is considered high risk and can't even do that. I suggest she walk a marathon's worth in our backyard, or in our bedroom. She doesn't care for either suggestion. We remain in the house, even as April begins to shift melted snow into soft ground, the boundaries of grass and of lawn and yard.

After lunch, Christine heads to the bedroom for a conference call, and our young ladies are packed with boots and coats and set loose in the backyard. Once the girls are outside, coats are abandoned, and Rose returns repeatedly to fill a container with water, to wash the caked dirt off their plastic water table. She climbs their metal play structure, surveying the yard. Aoife, too small to climb, hangs from the bars. I retreat to my desk and return to Julie Carr's *Sarah—Of Fragments and Lines* (2010), a book I found remarkable when I first opened it, and still do: "To write in order to leave, for good, the day." If we can leave today, somehow, might a new day begin?

I remember slipping Carson an envelope of poetry chapbooks on the day of the lecture: did I dream that as well?

One comparison I haven't been seeing through any of this is to the Bill Murray classic *Groundhog Day* (1993): the eight years, eight months, and sixteen days, according to the website *Wolf Gnards*, or ten full years, according to the late director Harold Ramis, that Murray's Phil Connors was trapped in his daily loop. As Phil soon discovered, there are things we have control over and things we don't. We can keep a physical distance from our friends, family, and neighbours, even as we attempt to check in through electronic or digital means. We can pressure our government representatives to do more, do different, do better. As well, we flail at homeschooling, finances, meal-planning. We wash our hands. We stay the fuck home. What is normal? We binge-watch television and try to remain as healthy and safe as possible.

We aren't at the point of dropping toasters into bathtubs, as Phil did at one point in the movie. We're hoping to forego that particular dark stretch of repeated days, aiming instead to launch directly from apathy into the myriad improvements that might be available. Get creative, inventive. Move forward. What do we have in the house for a craft project? Might we, like Phil, take up an instrument? Do we take up previously unaddressed tasks? Read a book? Might we attempt to assist someone in the neighbourhood, despite knowing we might never be acknowledged? It takes two or three days to work up to cleaning parts of the house. Toronto poet Andy Weaver mentions that he and his wife, Kelly, are taking the opportunity to re-watch most of the Marvel movies in order. The short-term impulses make way for long-term impulses. We work to maintain and even improve our surroundings, as well as ourselves. Christine works in our garden. I reorganize book storage. Christine filters out winter clothes from the children's dressers and closet to replace with their springwear, their summerwear. We don't know how long this might last. Bill Murray's character didn't either.

Eight to ten years. From both perspectives, the cycle appeared endless, until suddenly it wasn't. And who might we be once we finally emerge?

Most days we balance well enough, occasionally struggling simply to maintain, and not miss out on, another of Rose's virtual school sessions or Aoife's virtual "circle time" from her preschool. We attempt to keep a schedule of children and work. The mail from the front door; did you wash your hands?

Christine says she's seen articles referencing *Groundhog Day*—of course she has—but I haven't. Perhaps we're all in our isolations, utilizing the same references to arrive at the same conclusions, time after time after time. Is this, in fact, our predicted loop?

And then there is Toronto writer Lynn Crosbie, from her classic "Alphabet City," included in what deserved to be an award-winning collection, *Queen Rat: New and Selected Poems* (1998): "Like glass, sealed together with breath, our breath held to be blessed, something // we never forget."

The death tolls stagger. According to *The Hill*: "As of 3:00 pm Eastern time on April 16, there were 30,920 coronavirus deaths in the U.S. New York State accounted for 14,198—or 46 percent—of those deaths." Too many of these were preventable. How are we to comprehend the volume of those affected? Nursing homes are cleaned out, and one woman, two weeks after she was told her mother had died, still had no idea where her mother's body lay, most likely in a refrigerator truck. There is no death certificate, no funeral home, no follow-up. She can't get anyone to tell her. The nursing home won't even pick up the phone.

And through this, protests gain stream, as various groups push for an end to the shutdowns. Vancouver, Washington, California. Florida. The insanity. Dozens, even hundreds, gather. A handful of state governors push back, and President Trump tweets and endorses their recklessnesses. We should storm the capital, they say. How is this happening? Via Twitter, musician Richard Marx compares the situation to the difference between the smoking and non-smoking sections of airplanes, although one of the responses, suggesting the "peeing section of the pool," might better make the point.

Record, remember. Keep track. From Paul Celan's *Breathturn into Timestead: The Collected Later Poetry*, translated from the German and with commentary by Pierre Joris (2014):

THE NUMBERS, in league
with the images' doom
and counter-
doom.

Christine has always preferred Joris's translations of Celan to those of Michael Hamburger, translator of the Paul Celan collection I've had on my shelf since my twenties. I'll admit I haven't read enough Celan to properly know the difference between the two translation approaches, although one factor could be that Christine actually knows some German, whereas I do not. German is the language her mother knew first as a child in Winnipeg, before she was old enough to start school, and developed her English.

Poetry is impossible, some have said, after such willful negligence, after such willful death. As Pierre Joris writes on Celan as part of his introduction to the collection:

> He is a survivor of *khurbn* (to use Jerome Rothenberg's "ancient and dark word"), and his work is a constant bearing witness to those atrocities; even when it imagines a world beyond those historical limits, it remains *eingedenk* (to use Hölderlin's word), that is, mindful, conscious of said events.

Not that I would compare what Celan was responding to to this current pandemic. I don't wish to belittle or misrepresent either. While the Covid-19 pandemic might not have been preventable, it could certainly have been mitigated, keeping the death toll far lower. There are some important elements to Joris's sentence: "witness," "mindful," and "a world beyond." It is, as Celan's work displays so well, fully possible to be simultaneously attuned to all three of those ideas.

As American poet Matthew Minicucci @MattMinicucci tweets:

> Don't apologize for being productive.

> Don't apologize for being unproductive.

> Most of your productivity making bread and posting about it? Beg for mercy you monster.

To ensure physical distancing, Ottawa's National Capital Commission has announced it will close a stretch of Queen Elizabeth Drive to vehicles from April 18 to 26. For this "pilot project," a whole stretch of the driveway, which slides kilometres along the western length of the Rideau Canal, will be closed to all but emergency vehicles and foot traffic, ensuring locals can physically distance while out on required errands or exercise. Out for a walk. Many have called for similar closures in other urban centres, from New York to Toronto to Vancouver, asking that certain streets be closed off to traffic so pedestrians can walk without fear. Or with less fear, anyway.

It is a lovely stretch, and knowing this, the City of Ottawa has also requested that individuals not go out of their way to make this new walkway a destination.

Fiona Apple drops an album. The internet is, as they say, abuzz.

A CBC article on Vancouver writer and artist Douglas Coupland focuses on a project of postered slogans he's been releasing on Instagram, a project from 2011 that has been "activated by 2020." Each slogan is set in large block letters on a single-colour background, from the foreboding to the uplifting, including the specifically relevant "Everybody On Earth Is Feeling The Same Way As You."

> "That, more than anything, defines the present moment, that we're all in this together. There's no one who escapes this. Movie stars don't escape it. The one percent of the one percent, everybody is in it together," says Coupland. "And there's something wonderful that comes from that."

We're all living the same rainy day, he says, although that isn't entirely true. We aren't all in the same boat, someone offers, although we are in the same storm.

Prompted by a tweet by novelist Amy Jones, I lapse into the Sugarcubes, Björk's pre-solo band, called "the coolest band in the world" by *Rolling Stone* in 1988. I even used to have that first album: where did it go? My long-lost record collection, left temporarily with my ex-wife in the mid-1990s, that now sits in my eldest daughter's Aylmer, Quebec, living room. There are some good albums there. I hope she appreciates them.

On the homestead, the furnace explodes in my father's house, relocating him and his health care support, including my sister, to a neighbour's house. Everyone wears masks. Already the duct cleaners and furnace replacers are scheduled in shifts for their projection. It might still be a week or two before the cleaners manage to scrub down the layers of oil and smoke from the surfaces. Everyone, but for my father, is on edge. There is little, perhaps nothing, Christine or I can do from here. He says: just set me up in the workshop. His uninsulated machine shop, with concrete floor? To that, a clear no.

Canadian poet Lisa Pasold posts a photo of her neighbour's cactus plants, suddenly in bloom, with the hashtag #poetrykeepsmesane, along with a quote from something of mine. While I appreciate the gesture, I would think the flowering cactus provides more salve in her example than I ever could.

In lockdown, I ruminate upon my own bookshelves, moving back and forth between titles slipped from my non-fiction shelves, my poetry shelves, my trade comic shelves. *Avengers vs. X-Men*, or *Original Sin*. Books I haven't looked through in months, even years. From New Zealand poet Hera Lindsay Bird's self-titled debut (2016), the poem "Pain Imperatives," includes:

> The past is a bad invention that keeps on happening
> And it hurts to think about, like an unpaid bill
>
> It's the wind dragging the desert backwards at night
> & it burns you, like a little pastel whip

I picked this up during our last visit through London, after Christine and I emerged from an overnight train south, out of the Scottish Highlands. Might travel exist again? Is London still there? Was it all just a dream?

Via *Time* magazine, Margaret Atwood says, "It's the best of times, it's the worst of times. How you experience this time will be, in part, up to you." Hers is a practical list that presumes a certain amount of financial stability and comfort: how we should and could still access bookstores and check in with loved ones. Her article focuses very much on simply getting to the work at hand, but what if one hasn't the options to do so?

I take her advice with a grain of salt, aware of how privileged she is in such a situation, and our household as well, knowing so many are on the front lines, with fewer options for how they can deal with all of this. Her comments appear to be directed to so many of those going squirrelly at home in self-isolation, unable to work or do much at all. I think of my sister, dealing with the chaos of caregiving our father in our neighbour's house, and how long that might last before the homestead returns from the cleaners. Atwood writes:

> Finally, keep the faith. You can make it across that moat! Yes, this moment is scary and unpleasant. People are dying. People are losing their jobs and the feeling that they're in control of their lives, however cliff's-edge that control may have been. But if you aren't ill—and even if you have small children and feel your brain has been kidnapped—you're actually in a good place, comparatively speaking.
>
> You can enjoy this time, albeit at a pace somewhat less frenzied than it was when things were "normal." Many are questioning that pace—What was the hurry?—and deciding to live differently.

I would like to see those differences, although, as Mary Harris points out in an April 16 piece for *Slate*, we have neither exit strategies for reopening the economy nor returning to whatever "normal" is supposed to look like. Perhaps there is no such thing. As part of her piece, she interviews Ed Yong, a science writer for the *Atlantic*, who responds:

> I think the idea that life will be dramatically different is correct. You could argue that a failure of imagination has led us to the point we're currently at: where even people who've been thinking about this for a long time didn't foresee some of the stumbling points in America's past, like its inability to get a good diagnostic test up and running throughout the country in time.

It's going to take feats of imagination to steel ourselves—not just in terms of material resources and logistical plans, but also psychologically—for the idea that the summer, the rest of the year, maybe even longer, is going to be different.

I see someone post the poem "Red Squall," by Wanda Coleman, which includes: "There's no relief, but I refuse the flood."

It is strange to think that today should have been the Anansi Poetry Bash at the Manx Pub, as part of the spring edition of the Ottawa International Writers Festival, featuring: "*Roguelike* by Mathew Henderson, the much-anticipated follow-up to his acclaimed 2012 debut *The Lease*; John Elizabeth Stintzi's debut collection, *Junebat*, and Griffin Poetry Prize winner A. F. Moritz's twentieth collection, *As Far as You Know*." I might even have been at that. Where did I put my copies of those?

Instead, I watch as articles begin to appear saying President Trump and his supporters are in an emerging "death cult," willing to potentially sacrifice the lives of tens of thousands for the sake of reopening the economy. Ali Breland, in an April 4, 2020, article for *Mother Jones*, compares the current situation to cult leader Jim Jones's 1978 murder-suicide at Jonestown:

> "A narcissist was forced to take down hundreds of people because that community was less important to him than the truth that he personally represented," Zeller said on the phone, describing both Jones' decision to poison his followers, and Trump's musings about scrapping social distancing precautions. "Those were murders as well as suicides," Zeller explained of Jonestown. "Ultimately it was more important for Jones and some of the people at the top of the movement that they all go out rather than be taken down by outsiders."

My thoughts turn to mush. These essays turn to mush. Individual pieces, like the days themselves, begin to feel indistinguishable.

Today it is raining. Last week it was snowing. It will snow again.

There are such swings of the pendulum, from doomsday anxieties to the refusal to give in to those same anxieties. We're all in this together, they'll say, until someone else points out that, in fact, we are not. Swing, baby, swing.

Perhaps it is a matter of writing, of writing ourselves into, or back into, existence, something Montreal writer Nicole Brossard figured out a very long time ago. From her *Intimate Journal* (2004), translated by Barbara Godard:

25 March 1983

Everything's a question of framing in the landscape of the real, of montage and dissolve in memory, when a mental frame is transformed into a precise image of a woman in the process of writing. In contrast, you have to expect the real twice because there is no real(ity) except the science of being as an absolute necessity otherwise consciousness does not survive, invisible in the montage.

Is this all imaginary? Within hours, I find myself deep in Andrew Hurley's translation of Jorge Luis Borges's *The Book of Imaginary Beings* (2005), specifically this fragment of his entry on "The Jinn":

They make themselves visible at first as clouds or tall undefined pillars; then, according to their desire, they take the form of men, jackals, wolves, lions, scorpions, or serpents. Some are believers; others, infidels—heretics or atheists. Before a person kills a serpent, one should admonish it, in the name of the Prophet, to depart the chamber it has entered; it may be killed if it does not obey. Jinn are able to pass through thick walls or fly through the air or suddenly become invisible. "They often ascend to the confines of the lowest heaven," Lane tells us, "and there, listening to the conversation of the Angels respecting things decreed by God, obtain knowledge of futurity, which they sometimes impart to men, who, by means of talismans, or certain invocations, make them to serve the purposes of magical performances." Some scholars say that the Jinn (or one of them) built the pyramids of Egypt, and also, by order of Suleyman (Solomon), who knew the Most Great Name of god, the Temple of Jerusalem.

At *Literary Hub*, posted April 17, "An Argument for Slowing the F*ck Down with War and Peace: Natalie Adler on the Beauty of the Little Things." Adler writes on the ongoing emergencies, border walls, and climate change:

A recommendation for the disoriented: spend a day in a dark theater with Sergei Bondarchuk's 1968 opus adaptation of Leo Tolstoy's *War and Peace*, which is newly restored and in limited release around the country. Waiting for spring is obviously a perfect time for long Russian novels and binge watching costume dramas, but what makes *War and Peace* so perfect is that it offers a different way of experiencing time than we do today, incessantly scrolling through a nightmare news cycle without a moment to process the effects of nonstop atrocity. In *War and Peace*, news emerges like gossip bubbling from the mouths of partygoers, or with the urgency of a letter that carries information that may already be out of date. Clocking in just over four hundred minutes, the four-part film is the right balm for our hyper-accelerated times.

If this is but a single moment, a single day, stretched out. Along similar lines, I begin to listen to later Brian Eno: long, tonal structures that provide ambient foundation to this lengthy stretch. I seek out, and the internet provides: *Thursday Afternoon* (1985) and *New Space Music* (2014). I find his music soothing, having first come to it through listening to David Bowie. These days, Eno's music is the difference of jam, one might say, on an otherwise bare slice of bread.

Today is Sunday, and Christine heads out to collect pre-ordered soil and other supplies in a parking-lot pickup. She constructs our Victory

Garden, attempting to increase the size of what we'd planted last year. Why do we have so many pumpkin seeds? she asks. Why do we have so many beans? Yesterday, we even managed to assemble the new garden beds she'd ordered long before these lockdowns began.

The squirrels have already pulled and devoured her tulip bulbs, all her planted garlic bulbs.

The days of the week: weekday mornings now include Zoom offerings at 9:00 a.m. from Aoife's preschool. Wednesdays at 11:00 a.m., Rose's class does the same. Every second Friday, I head to the farm.

I attempt to remain in motion. Motion, as opposed to stasis, which might quickly develop into an apathetic immobility. Siri Hustvedt, from *Living, Thinking, Looking* (2012): "Living is movement. Thoughts are in motion, and when I think, my body thinks too. While writing I find the words not only in my mind but in the feeling of my fingers on the keyboard. When I'm stuck, I stand up and walk around the room, and walking often jogs the sentence loose."

Where was the bookstore I picked up the Hustvedt collection? It was inside a mall somewhere in London, England, during our honeymoon. I remember a piano set out for the public to play. Might this have been by a tube station?

Toronto announces a phased reopening plan, as do Georgia, Tennessee, and South Carolina. Is this a good idea? Better to be fluid, akin to Eno's sustained note. It swells, contracts, twists.

Rose beelines into my office and requests I assist her as she puts on her cat costume. Fifteen minutes later, Aoife requests I assist her to put on the same costume. "I'm going to be a good kitty," she says. Rose is now dressed as a witch. They are preparing a potion.

●

Over at *Slate*, Vanessa Chang writes of "The Post-Pandemic Style," reflecting on how previous outbreaks have shifted ideas of architecture and public space. "Just as those scourges scarred and then reshaped cities, so will ours," she writes.

> The flu pandemic killed tens of millions from 1918–20. Six cholera pandemics in the 19th century alone laid waste to hundreds of thousands of lives. Between 1810 and 1815, aggravated by overcrowding and filthy living conditions, tuberculosis was the cause of more than 25 percent of deaths in New York City. Robert Koch's discovery of the contagious tubercle bacillus in 1882 gave rise to the sanatorium movement in Europe and the United States. Designed to house, treat, and isolate patients, these institutions emphasized strict hygiene and ample exposure to sunlight and air. Before the development of medications for tuberculosis, its treatment was environmental. These clinical environments inspired the new modern architecture. As the Swiss architect Le Corbusier declared, "A house is only habitable when it is full of light and air."

How will this pandemic shift how we design to move through the world? Already, lines of intervalled tape at checkouts and bank machines, with plastic shields protecting cashiers and bank tellers. Vast improvements in air quality have been cited for weeks, such as the *Guardian* offered on April 11, with reports "by Hannah Ellis-Petersen in Delhi, Rebecca Ratcliffe in Bangkok, Sam Cowie in São Paulo, Joe Parkin Daniels in Bogotá and Lily Kuo in Beijing." Photographs highlighting the differences between now and even six months ago are startling, turning a rust-coloured air a bright blue. For example:

In Delhi, air quality index (AQI) levels are usually a severe 200 on a good day (anything above 25 is deemed unsafe by World Health Organization). During peak pollution periods last year they soared well into a life-threatening 900 and sometimes off the measurable scale. But as Delhi's 11m registered cars were taken off the roads and factories and construction were ground to a halt, AQI levels have regularly fallen below 20. The skies are suddenly a rare, piercing blue. Even the birdsong seems louder.

Once the world begins to reopen, how will these shifts continue to present themselves? How many might remain?

I spend a good part of my morning composing letters. Every time I write a letter now, I am conscious of the trope of letters home from front-line American Civil War soldiers, all of which seem to begin "Dearest Martha" (Civil War wives, as we know, were all named Martha). Were there really such letters composed by Civil War–era soldiers? I have a half-brother in Florida who finds it baffling I can barely do anything more than use my phone for basic texting, prompting me to seek out parchment paper and a quill so I might compose him one of these eighteenth-century missives in the appropriate style. *Dearest brother*, I write, *I am far from home and wishing you the best of health.*

In an April 17 article in the *Tyee*, Andrew MacLeod quotes Dr. Bonnie Henry, B.C.'s provincial health officer: "'It's really important to recognize we are not at the end of our beginning yet.'"

What does that even mean? Japan is apparently bracing itself for a Covid-19 second wave. Ebb and flow, akin to a river, running across the surface of the entire planet. Repeatedly, articles and tweets and emails point out how this crisis highlights what should be the focal points of our attentions: climate change and economic disparities. There are increasing articles on just how much a guaranteed annual income will reduce poverty and actually stimulate economic activity, the opposite of what those who are against the idea seem to be arguing. But what are these arguments?

•

I was born, and subsequently live, in the City of Ottawa. We've been Capital City ever since Queen Victoria decided to choose a centre off the waterways—Toronto, Kingston, Montreal—for fear of further American attempts at invasion. The 1775 American invasion of Quebec and the siege of Montreal, for example, or the burning of York (a town later renamed Toronto) as part of the War of 1812. Ours was the city a young Elizabeth Smart escaped and barely referenced in her writing, and one that André Alexis might have relocated away from but never entirely left. Ours a town once known as the most dangerous in the commonwealth, shifting from a Victorian rail and lumber town to a government bureaucracy as layered and multiple as sediment.

One hears of food banks feeding more than usual, with lineups into the thousands in San Antonio, Texas. I suspect Ottawa is buffered from any greater financial calamity, although certainly not free from any potential effects. During the Great Depression, the citizens of Ottawa were protected from much of the crisis, working in essential jobs for the federal government.

There is a shooting in rural Nova Scotia, with more than a dozen dead initially reported. The final tally ends up at twenty-three dead across fifty kilometres, most of them strangers to the assailant. The worst shooting in the province's history. We are at the beginning of this, but even if and when the shooter's motivations are uncovered, they will be impossible to comprehend.

I have an email exchange with Ottawa poet Michael Dennis this morning, one of two poet friends I know with a recent cancer diagnosis. His is the terminal charge. He says: "I won't be writing anything else."

Saskatchewan's provincial NDP leader, Ryan Meili, renews his medical licence and returns to the front lines. Multiple retired medical workers have been reported doing the same, including a member of the European royal families.

The *Guardian* reports that "Carol Ann Duffy has launched an international poetry project with major names including Imtiaz Dharker, Roger McGough and Ian McMillan, as a response to the coronavirus pandemic."

> The former poet laureate hopes the project, entitled Write Where We Are Now, "will provide an opportunity for reflection and inspiration in these challenging times, as well as creating a living record of what is happening as seen through our poets' eyes and ears, in their gardens or garrets."

I like the idea of the "living record," archiving an important aspect through language of such a period of uncertainty, upheaval, and ever-changing statistics. I'll admit, I myself haven't written anything in the way of poetry since this began, but most of that is due to my focus on this, on these notes. The canvas I work on is vast, and too large to hold what any single page, any single poem, at least in my comprehension or ability, might be able to contain. Although, as Elisa Gabbert writes in *The Word Pretty* (2018):

> So let's talk about the difference between poetry and prose: a difference so often belabored but rarely to much satisfaction. This or that critic, as a way of calling a poem basic, often balks at its being "just prose chopped up into lines." Reader, this statement may sound radical at first, but it couldn't be more obvious: Poetry is just prose chopped up into lines. I mean this to be final, categorical, and no slight on poetry.

I mean, I don't need to agree with her to appreciate her thinking. She's right, but the answer is also more complicated. And yet, I wouldn't know exactly how to describe either one without immediately citing a list of exceptions. *Yes, but...* I begin. Already the music begins to play my theory off-stage. Wait, am I done? Here I am, writing. Is this all poetry—or prose, for that matter—is?

•

"There are more important things than living," Texas lieutenant governor Dan Patrick says to Fox News's Tucker Carlson, explaining his push to re-open the economy. I don't even know how to process this: there are those who see human life as disposable, compared to what they see as the needs of the economy. There are terrible, awful, stupid people everywhere, and I know certain of them manage positions that allow them platforms, and levels of power that are frightening. I'm baffled at this dismissal of human life, and it's exactly the opposite of everything Western media culture has taught us to believe. From World War II films to *Star Trek* to Westerns (which might all be the same genre, really): Leave no one behind.

It seems so blatant: how the working poor will bear the brunt of these decisions. Utterly heartless, utterly cruel. In *The Spirit of Prague and Other Essays* (1994), Ivan Klíma wrote: "Power is soulless and it is derived from soullessness. It builds on it and draws its strength from it. Soullessness keeps company with fear. People who have given up their souls have only a body, and it is the body they are terrified for."

I've been seeking out my copy of a collection of essays by Alice Notley, who I feel might have something appropriate to offer in response to this era. How does one write, or even continue, in the face of such arrogance, such culturally self-defeating attempts to keep money flowing into the coffers of the already-wealthy? The more one has accumulated, I've heard it theorized, the more one becomes terrified of losing it all. The more one is willing to sacrifice another to maintain the status quo.

Christine and I were discussing it yesterday—this American mythology built, essentially, around libertarianism: a notion of individual liberty that becomes twisted to the point that a lockdown for the sake of a global pandemic and the continued safety and health of the American population is regarded as trampling on personal rights. How the government is out to get you, clearly. A disease created in a lab so they could take away your rights, your guns, your freedoms. Stories emerging of those who have died from Covid-19, including many individuals who had declared the outbreak a hoax, or no worse than the flu. The dozens of pastors across the Bible Belt who have died after previously dismissing public health recommendations, refusing to shut down services and downplaying the need for physical distancing. By the end of April, *The Independent* reports: "As many as 30 church leaders from the nation's largest African American Pentecostal denomination have now been confirmed to have died in the outbreak, as members defied public health warnings to avoid large gatherings to prevent transmitting the virus." Fox News editorials and round tables spent weeks perpetuating dismissals of such preventative measures, but behind the scenes, executives and staff did everything they could to work from home. There are those who would call this, too, a hoax. How does one protect anything against such willful ignorance? Not that we're free of this in Canada, either.

I've been cleaning out further parts of my home office—a mound of books, chapbooks, and papers at the base of a bookshelf, as well as a corner overrun with paper archive, eventually set to be organized and sent off to the University of Calgary. If you can imagine it, I already have some ninety banker's boxes worth of literary archive sitting in their stores. And yet, there is no sign of that Alice Notley title.

Instead, I spend part of the morning rereading Maggie Helwig's debut essay collection, *Apocalypse Jazz* (1993), reminded of just how damned smart she is, writing on apocalypse, Bob Dylan, Northrop Frye, and Japanese literature post-Hiroshima. Here she is on Shakespeare's *The Tempest*:

> We are all, necessarily, aware that the material world is an ambiguous thing. It may be brought to our service, even destroyed by us, but never willingly so; it is, for us, a strange combination of ally, slave and enemy. Or, to put it in terms that an Elizabethan would have understood, the Fall of man from Eden

brought about a corresponding fall in nature; we, the cosmos, and our relationship with it are profoundly "out of joint." And only when we are redeemed will the world be redeemed as well.

Roughly a decade after this collection appeared in print, Helwig was ordained an Anglican priest. There are times I envy her parishioners their access to her insights.

I move through an essay by the late Kevin Killian from *Biting the Error: Writers Explore Narrative* (2004): "How did I write a whole book? I'm trying to remember."

"In the beginning," Paul Auster writes, to open his *Report from the Interior* (2013),

everything was alive. The smallest objects were endowed with beating hearts, and even the clouds had names. Scissors could walk, telephones and teapots were first cousins, eyes and eyeglasses were brothers. The face of the clock was a human face, each pea in your bowl had a different personality, and the grille on the front of your parents' car was a grinning mouth with many teeth. Pens were airships. Coins were flying saucers. The branches were arms. Stones could think, and God was everywhere.

And yet, an article floats through from the University of Guelph, a news item from their website: "U of G Expert Says Pandemic Response Proves Changes to Protect Earth Are Possible." The article focuses on poet Madhur Anand, "a University of Guelph expert in global change ecology and sustainability": "What Anand thinks all of us can learn from this unique year is that rapid societal changes are possible and that social norms can change."

I'm going to hold on to that. Might it be enough?

Avery Trufelman—@trufelman—posts to Twitter: "In the 1300s Italians believed that people with the plague died within 37 days. So people and shipments coming to Venice had to wait outside the city gates for 40 days before they could enter. The Italian word for 40 is quaranta. Hence 'quarantined.'" When I offer this new discovery to Christine, she says she already knew that. I didn't. Has it been forty days? March 13 was our children's last day of school and preschool prior to March break, from which we quickly learned there would be a two-week break from school to follow, and we had a visitor stop by on March 14, which makes April 23 our fortieth consecutive day of self-quarantine.

Writing from, and of, as Dani Couture, also via Twitter, coins it, "the small hours of self-isolation."

Forty days and forty nights. April 23, 2020. Forty days since we had any interaction with anyone outside our immediate circle. What have we learned through the process so far? Just how far have we come, and how much further have we to go?

I'm rereading Brian Michael Bendis's graphic novel *Age of Ultron*. Perhaps this isn't the time for such apocalyptic stories, although where else do I turn, now that new comics are no longer appearing weekly? Depicting the end of the world. Depicting the devastation. Perhaps I should move in a different direction. Or perhaps through other stretches of reading, such as Bendis's incredible run on *The Avengers*.

If one wishes to regain and retain ground, one could do no better than through Don McKay, a poet who maintains a foot in Glengarry County, even from his home base of Newfoundland. Listen to this excerpt from his *Deactivated West 100* (2005):

How can you be lost? When the incredulity fades, when the anger damps down, when the fear diminishes from clamour to drone, the question may be open to receive other inflections, other echoes. The question may finally *be* a question. You think of Hamlet telling Horatio that there are more things in heaven and earth than are dreamt of in his philosophy, how entire readings of the play can depend on which word receives the emphasis. Sitting on your stump in the middle of a clearcut-to-come, you reflect on the paradox embedded in the common expression 'to get lost': you can't get lost any more than you can fall asleep. Lostness gets you; sleep gathers you inward to itself. But being lost—can a person dwell in such a space, somewhere outside the ubiquity of plans, the falling boundaries and logging roads projected into the future? Deep in your backpack, Tomas Tranströmer murmurs of that nearly-discovered country between wakefulness and sleep, of Schubert's music catching an entire life in a few ordinary chords, of a clearing which can only be found by someone who is lost.

Again, we speak of silence, and the boundaries of sleep. I think back to those first few days after September 11, those first few hours after the collapse of the towers. There were such unnerving silences broadcast across my Somerset Street West–facing front window. Such silences throughout Chinatown, and further east, into Centretown proper. We were glued to our televisions, afraid of what might come next. Office workers sent home, the Rideau Centre shut down, Parliament Hill evacuated. Wondering if Parliament Hill might be a target. Wondering whether—if something did happen here in Ottawa—I lived close enough to be affected. We could walk around, and interact, but everyone was shocked into muteness. We broadcast our silence, increasing it. Making it larger, until we were finally forced to speak. For our own safety. Our own sanity. How we had to return, led out of silence and back into speech.

The twinge in my stomach a few days later, as flights resumed, and I saw that first airplane soar overhead.

Toronto poet Paul Vermeersch tweets a question about a particular kind of Ontario Gothic, requesting works where the gothic emerges, in part, through water. He references Al Purdy and Catherine Graham as examples, although I'm immediately reminded of Margaret Atwood's novel *Surfacing* (1972). More than a decade ago, I composed an essay on Phil Hall's ongoing "Ontario Gothic," wondering if some of the poems he has been writing over the years since, in his house on the shores of Otty Lake, near Perth, might fit with Paul's query. I think of this, from the end of Phil's *Guthrie Clothing—The Poetry of Phil Hall, a Selected Collage* (2015):

I have the dates & details wrong   I refuse to understand

I trust my tin-ear / this blind stupid hand gropes

Over the past few weeks, I feel as though we've become more attuned to the weather. Perhaps it's the time of year, but the cycle of snow, the warm sun, the rain, the snow again, makes an effect, far more than it might have. On *Late Night with Seth Meyers*, Trevor Noah says he doesn't see anything different when he goes onto his Twitter feed, as though the world hasn't changed and isn't on lockdown, although I very much see the opposite. Throughout my feed, everything is heightened, from the reluctance to share personal good news, to the many personal essays and news articles on aspects of the global crisis, to so many online who are simply attempting to reach everyone—anyone—through the screen.

I still haven't located that collection of essays by Alice Notley I'd been looking for. Perhaps I imagined its existence. Perhaps it was a dream I once had. If I sleep, I might find it. As well, I find myself moving further into Brian Eno, *An Ending (Ascent) Long Version* (1983). The internet abides. Apparently it is William Shakespeare's birthday, born this day in 1564. Did you know that he shares a birthday with the English painter J. M. W. Turner (1775), Nobel Prize–winning German scientist and theoretical physicist Max Karl Ernst Ludwig Planck (1858), Russian-American novelist Vladimir Nabokov (1899), and Prime Minister (and Nobel Prize–winner) Lester B. Pearson (1897)? That's quite a list. Not to mention Shirley Temple (1928), Lee Majors (1940), and Sandra Dee (1942).

Rereading Paul Celan prompted me to write a letter to Mark Goldstein, which I am finally putting the finishing touches on today. This prompts me, as well, into his own Celan-influenced poetry collection *Tracelanguage: A Shared Breath* (2010). I write to Mark: "Going through some Paul Celan today; Christine and I discussing the difference between the translations by Hamburger vs. Pierre Joris (which she prefers). The difference of language, how she suggests Hamburger normalizes, where Joris is more attuned to the language-aspect of the German. More open to it." And even before I manage to seal up the envelope, Goldstein, in his own way, responds, through *Tracelanguage*:

> Your absence testifies
> to the nudity of each beginning—
> a kingless burden
> in death.

Yesterday afternoon, Rose wandered into my office with a feather dust-er, declaring the room too dusty. I told her I had been waiting for her the whole time and didn't wish to take such opportunity away from her. She is six, after all. She happily dusted numerous bookshelves before she decided she had done enough and left for her bath. Bumping into a small stack of books, she uncovers my copy of Ali Smith's *The Book Lover* (2006), an anthology of "some of the favourite reading of writ-ers, not just current but over a lifetime." Smith's selections move from novel excerpts to travel journals to memoir to poetry to short stories. The whole world lives in this collection. Or, at least, an element of Ali Smith's whole world. She writes in her introduction: "That's the thing about books. They're alive on their own terms. Reading is like travel-ling with an argumentative, unpredictable good friend. It's an endless open exchange."

Included in the collection is a stunning postcard-sized story by Lyd-ia Davis, in which much occurs but nothing is accomplished; selections by Clarice Lispector, Italo Calvino, Simone de Beauvoir, Gertrude Stein, Helen Oyeyemi, and a few dozen others. Moving through the collection, I pause at the poem "Hymn to Iris" by Alice Oswald, which includes:

Put your hands
Put your heaven-taken shape down
On the ground.

In a piece for the *Paris Review*, posted April 22, under the title "The Writer's Obligation," Wayne Koestenbaum offers:

The writer's obligation in the age of X is to play with words and to keep playing with them—not to deracinate or deplete them, but to use them as vehicles for discovering history, recovering wounds, reciting damage, and awakening conscience.

There is so much fear. I have an itch in my throat. Should I do something? Should I call my doctor? Might I pick up the virus simply by going in? What if it's strep? Last year, Christine's untreated strep evolved into rheumatic fever, which her multiple doctors now theorize triggered her stroke. By doing and saying nothing, am I making this worse? She is immune-compromised, after all. The fear overtakes reason. There is no reason. There are no days.

Once every week or two, I make for the post office. I pick up milk, bread, and whatever else might be possible at our local Shopper's Drug Mart. The few people in the store have masks, and most of the staff are wearing gloves. We maintain our distances.

Today, a mixture of stunned and sad to hear of the death, two days earlier, of my friend and early mentor, Fredericton poet and Broken Jaw Press publisher Joe Blades. I'd checked in with him via email not three weeks ago, and he responded within a day or two, writing: "Trying to hang in there. not easy with need for groceries and stuff. My bank branch closed, but credit union open. so many places closed. My father died on 21 march with many resultant complications for mother and us. today i received a COVID-19 emergency bursary from UNB."

A month after his father died, so has he. I am gutted that my friend is dead.

Another funeral deferred, and by the time the obituary is published, cremation has already occurred. A memorial, it offers, will take place at a later time.

Michael Cavuto, *Country Poems* (2020): "delusions / are the things of poems."

In the *New York Times Magazine* on April 23, Gabrielle Hamilton writes on the events and repercussions, including emotional, financial, and staffing, surrounding her decision to shut down her twenty-year-old Manhattan restaurant, Prune, mere hours before New York City mayor Bill de Blasio declared a city-wide Covid-19 shutdown.

> I have been shuttered before. With no help from the government, Prune has survived 9/11, the blackout, Hurricane Sandy, the recession, months of a city water-main replacement, online reservations systems—you still have to call us on the telephone, and we still use a pencil and paper to take reservations! We've survived the tyranny of convenience culture and the invasion of Caviar, Seamless and Grubhub. So I'm going to let the restaurant sleep, like the beauty she is, shallow breathing, dormant. Bills unpaid. And see what she looks like when she wakes up—so well rested, young all over again, in a city that may no longer recognize her, want her or need her.

And still, there is talk of sleep. I remember the big blackout. August 14, 2003, a power outage that took out parts of Ontario as well as wide swaths the northeastern and midwestern United States. Buffalo, Toronto, Ottawa, New York City. I made my way to an ex-girlfriend's condo across the provincial bridge, since Quebec still had power. It took us an hour to find a restaurant that didn't have a lineup the length of a further hour. And yet, there was something remarkable about standing, post-dusk, on Somerset Street West at the O-Train bridge, from within a capital city set solely to natural light.

A statistic floats by that says that some 60 per cent of businesses in Toronto would not survive if the shutdown lasts three months or more.

There is talk of reopening, although carefully. There have already been those who have pointed out that if you complain that the shutdowns should remain in place, you should first clarify whether or not you still have employment, and access to income. Where are we now? Forty-two days since our lockdown officially began. Since I turned fifty. Since Gabrielle Hamilton shuttered the gates.

Ecuadorian-American writer Bailey Cohen Vera—@BaileyC213—writes on Twitter: "I write a single email and it becomes tomorrow."

Beware, as someone else writes, the memory of proximity to living things. In *Canadian Art*, Michèle Pearson Clarke writes on "Isolation Portraits," of photographers taking portraits of their friends in isolation, akin to Stephen Brockwell's photography project. To introduce her interview with photographer Alyssa Bistonath, Clarke writes:

> But the doorstep portrait is not new. As Didier Aubert notes in a 2009 *Visual Studies* article, traditionally such images have unambiguous things to say about access, intrusion and the white, liberal, middle-class gaze—all issues which are deeply embedded in the documentary approach. Though Aubert was mostly writing about projects that sought to document poverty and rural life, these current isolation portraits traffic in the same transformation of private family life into a constructed public performance for a larger audience. The dynamics differ though: in these threshold quarantine spaces, we see not people asserting agency by restricting access to some other intimate visual truth of their lives, but people seeking momentary respite from the overwhelming reconstitution of time and space that makes up life under pandemic conditions. Access has been otherwise revoked, and intrusion appears quite welcome.

Bistonath responds: "But for me, the essential element is capturing intimate portraits of my friends while maintaining the distance necessary to keep us safe." The photographs acknowledge the shift in purpose and perspective, and the world changing in real time. The portraits are intimate, but as close as is possible, at least for the time being. But for how long?

Montreal poet Stephanie Bolster responds to my email on the death of Joe Blades, saying that even though she didn't know him well, she and her husband were affected by the news in ways she found unexpected. Joe wasn't that much older than she or I, which I suspect is a factor, but Christine suggests it's the crisis itself: one more thing on top of one more thing. She's right, of course. Concurrently, the *Boston Globe* runs the headline "Sunday's *Boston Globe* Runs 21 Pages of Death Notices as Coronavirus Continues to Claim Lives." William Wan, Carolyn Y. Johnson, and Joel Achenbach reported last week in the *Washington Post*:

> By the end of the week, residents in Georgia will be able to get their hair permed and nails done. By Monday, they will be cleared for action flicks at the cineplex and burgers at their favorite greasy spoon.
>
> And it will almost certainly lead to more novel coronavirus infections and deaths.

We've been under lockdown long enough that the expected ways of speaking on it, and speaking to it, fall away. At nearly six weeks, we enter into uncharted territory. In some corners, reopenings begin, even as polls show that the larger percentage of the population is concerned about opening too early.

Christine is in the bedroom, talking to her father on the phone. The children are downstairs, watching *Nature Cat*. The sun is out, although tomorrow's forecast calls for rain. We will have to send our young ladies outside today. What else can one say of silence? In an essay on the subject of "No" in *A Handbook of Disappointed Fate* (2018), Anne Boyer writes: "Silence is as often conspiracy as it is consent. A room of otherwise lively people saying nothing, staring at a figure of authority, is silence as the inchoate of a now-initiated *we won't.*"

Refusal, which is only sometimes a kind of poetry, does not have to be limited to poetry, and turning the world upside down, which is often a kind of poetry, doesn't have to be limited to words. Words are useful for upending the world in that they are cheap, ordinary, portable, and generous, and they don't mess us up too badly if we use them wrong, not like matches or machetes, but poetry is made up of ideas and figurations and tropes and syntaxes as much as it is made up of words. We can make a poetry without language because language as the rehearsal material of poetry has made the way for another poetry, that of objects, actions, environments and their arrangement. This is not saying to be a poet means you can only rehearse turning over the world: now try putting the chair on your head.

That, certainly, is a different kind of silence. Silence, as absence, comes in multiple forms, in multiple levels and flavours. Sound forms about silence, thereby giving it its shape. As Fanny Howe wrote of St. Francis of Assisi, and a period of six months through which his movements are unrecorded, in *The Needle's Eye: Passing through Youth* (2016): "It is possible that Francis, like others, fell in love with the silence of the desert, with the gardens and fruits and palm trees and fountains and marble buildings, sidereal skies."

Ours is an alternate silence, one that emerges through agreement, the terms of lockdown, and social distancing, but one that brings with it an absence of regular interaction. And yet, we exist as a household of four-plus-cat who haven't torn each other apart, content and comfortable in our isolations. We arc fortunate in this, I know. But we have further to go. In many ways, Boyer is the perfect companion for lockdown, for her steadfast refusals and defiant stance on isolations, disappointment, and imagination.

Earlier today, via CNN: "Pentagon Officially Releases UFO Videos." The article, with associated videos, reports: "The Pentagon has officially released three short videos showing 'unidentified aerial phenomena' that had previously been released by a private company." Excuse me? I'm not sure I have the capacity for this.

The videos show what appear to be unidentified flying objects rapidly moving while recorded by infrared cameras. Two of the videos contain service members reacting in awe at how quickly the objects are moving. One voice speculates that it could be a drone.

On the blog for the Munster Literature Centre in Cork, Ireland, "Writer & Editor, Sarah Byrne, shares a weekly series of personal essays on her favourite writer, Paul Celan, to mark the fiftieth anniversary of his death in April 2020." They're remarkable essays, sweeping through Celan in a structure reminiscent of Anne Carson, managing to bring multiple thoughts, sequences, and references into her tightly packed lyric. She writes in her series debut, "In Praise of Version":

> I'm trying my best to go in a circle so I can make a line for you, to paraphrase Moran in Beckett's *Molloy*. The two hours I mentioned that I was in love with happen somewhere in the middle of this story. Hegel thought that there were two types of time: Greek and modern. The future has already completed but that is different from it being pre-set.

That's a lot to unpack. And I, too, am both composing in circles and in a straight line, attempting the temporal from the timeless expanse of home office under lockdown, our two small children floating in and out of my office making requests. Occasionally, Rose will use the choral thread from *Frozen II*'s "Into the Unknown" as a call-and-response, to discover where her sister is in the house. She wanders the hallway and into the kitchen, waiting for Aoife's reply, so she may find her.

Christine responds to my burrowing throughout my office and out into the rest of the house for that elusive Alice Notley collection. What was the name of that book? she asks. What did it look like? Is this what you're looking for? She holds up her phone to show me the cover. I had the cover correct but was off with the title. In case she comes across it, she says. I think, given the grousing I've been doing around not knowing where my copy is, she's half-considering ordering me a replacement copy. Perhaps then I'll stop complaining. There is nothing worse than losing a book, especially when I know where nearly everything else in our library is, even if only roughly.

Aoife's is an Irish name. As I wrote as part of her birth announcement: "How does one reconcile an Irish first name with a Scottish surname?" There's Irish on Christine's McNair side, so it's fine, really. When researching the name, I became quite partial to Aoife MacMurrough (c. 1145–88), who often fought on behalf of her husband, Strongbow. MacMurrough was sometimes known as Red Eva (Irish: Aoife Rua). Her descendants include "all the monarchs of Scotland since Robert I (1274–1329) and all those of England, Great Britain and the United Kingdom since Henry IV (1367–1413); and, apart from Anne of Cleves, all the queen consorts of Henry VIII." It's still the third most popular girl's name for babies born in Ireland, and one online source said the name means "beautiful, radiant, joyful." "Known as the greatest woman warrior in the world, Aoife was the mother of Cuchulainn's only son, Connlach. Aoife Dearg ('Red Aoife') was a daughter of a king of Connacht who had her marriage arranged by St. Patrick himself." Right now, ours sings from the hallway of the main floor, trailing off down the stairs. Unlike Rose, a more flailing and expressive young lady, Aoife is even-tempered until she isn't, providing a fire and fury that becomes difficult to contain. But, after all, she is only four.

Rose pulls out the craft supplies that Christine recently purchased, which they ransack. They asked if they could, and I said yes, not understanding what it was they were asking. A bag containing dozens of plastic googly-eyes dumped across their bedroom floor, and every pipe cleaner and scrap of construction paper and cardboard that Christine had set aside pulled apart and opened. Over the days that follow, I see plastic eyes all over the house, scattered in corners of just about every room. Using a glue stick, Rose covers an empty chocolate-milk carton with eyes for a noisemaker, parading our hallway with her new shaker. All I can think of are those Biblical depictions of angels with one thousand eyes. From Ezekiel, Book 10: 10-14:

As for their appearance, all four had the same form, like a wheel within a wheel.

When they moved, they would go in any of the four directions, without turning as they moved. For wherever the head faced, the cherubim would go in that direction, without turning as they moved.

Their entire bodies, including their backs, hands, and wings, were full of eyes all around, as were their four wheels.

I heard the wheels being called "the whirling wheels."

Each of the cherubim had four faces: the first face was that of a cherub, the second that of a man, the third that of a lion, and the fourth that of an eagle.

Today, April 29, NPR.org offers that "[m]ore Americans have now died from the coronavirus in less than two months than in the entire nine years of the Vietnam war—more than 58,000. But the United States crossed another threshold Tuesday—1 million known coronavirus cases." These numbers exist even as some states begin to open. States begin to open, and employers threaten that those who refuse to come to work won't be eligible for unemployment. To those numbers, NPR adds a frightening perspective: "That is nearly one-third of all the world's known coronavirus cases. To put the enormity of that into context, the U.S.'s 328 million people is just over 4% of the world's population."

In a related thread, CTV News provides that Canada hosts 27,590 active cases, with 19,879 recovered and 2,904 deceased.

Singing loudly to herself, Rose shakes her angel chocolate-milk shaker as she descends into our finished basement. What might an outsider make of these associations I think to connect? In Srikanth Reddy's *Underworld Lit* (2020), through which he explores a variety of cultures' books of the dead via lyric memoir, he writes:

> Over the long twentieth century, countless schoolchildren, mental patients, prison inmates, and remote tribal peoples peered into Rorschach's dark stains around the globe. The popular artist Andrew Warhol painted gold, violet, sea-green, and pink inkblots large enough to walk into. Allied military psychologists administered the exam to high-ranking German officials awaiting execution at Nuremberg. Presumably they wanted to learn something about the psychopathology of every-day likeness. They showed their test subjects the Father Card, the Mother Card, and various other black marks that common-ly evoke animals, flowers, sexual organs, and so on. As of late, I've been seeing them everywhere: an oil spill in the gulf, the figure in the carpet, a stain on a shroud, a blur on a seam. Pro-jective assessments may take any number of forms, or, more properly speaking, forms of formlessness.

I see a poem float by on Twitter, by Portuguese poet Fernando Pes-soa, dated August 27, 1930, that includes:

My wife, whose name is Solitude,
Keeps me from being glum.

By the end of April, *Vanity Fair* offers to explore "Why Poetry Is Having a Moment Amid the Global Quarantine." I suspect I might know the answer, but I open the link. Quoting Ross Gay, Keziah Weir writes:

> "Why are poems circulating at this moment?" he asks. "Because they're necessary. Like Audre Lorde says, poetry is not a luxury. They circulate in moments of need, and moments of need are not necessarily moments of trouble. Moments of need are also moments of joy." Gay is often asked for poems—by the kids he coaches in basketball, by local groups doing a planting. In the last two months, he says, "People haven't said, 'Could you write a poem for this moment?' More people have said, 'We need a poem.'"

On April 30, Nunavut confirms its first case of Covid-19 in the north Baffin community of Pond Inlet, with the individual "in isolation and doing well," according to the chief health official. Within days, their cases return to zero.

Toronto publisher Coach House Books runs an informal contest via its Twitter feed, seeking the best "quarantine beard." What I see of the examples-to-date seem remarkably thin, so I snap a selfie and send it along. A few days later, apparently I've won, with a copy of their newly published Marion Poschmann novel, *The Pine Islands*, already en route to my doorstep. Translated by Jen Calleja, the novel follows a mythology of beards, hence the pandemic-ready contest. I spend the following twenty minutes parading my "award-winning beard" around our house, disappointed by how little my household has chosen to respond. I take to social media instead.

The other night on *Late Night with Seth Meyers,* he mentions a study done suggesting a large percentage of couples learning something of the other for the first time during these isolations, something we haven't encountered, despite some six weeks of lockdown. What else is there to know? I'll admit to being a bit jealous, although neither of us is that secretive. I suspect these studies might be done more with couples who both work extended hours outside the home. I've always worked from home, and Christine had two different year-long maternity leaves, as well as last year's seven months of medical leave. She was only beginning to return to working outside the house when this pandemic hit. I think we know well enough, although, as she offers, we might be reminded of things that annoy us about the other. Have I been warned?

How does one mourn in the midst of a crisis? My father succumbed to amyotrophic lateral sclerosis on May 1, some fifteen months after his initial diagnosis. They could not wake him up. He was already gone, but we spent the day waiting for his breathing to stop, removing his BiPAP machine to see if he could breathe on his own, and replacing it if he was. With his pacemaker, even a heartbeat wouldn't have told us anything. At mid-morning, his oxygen levels were at 40 per cent.

He went to sleep in April and woke up dead in May. It sounds reminiscent of some traditional English nursery rhyme, most of which were around death, disease, or religious persecution; a *Mental Floss* article wrote of "London Bridge Is Falling Down" as "the alleged destruction of London Bridge at the hands of Olaf II of Norway some time in the early 1000s." It is always curious how these short lyrics sung to children to engage in play or to put them to sleep so often emerged out of warnings, trauma, and lessons hard-won.

Never mind the prior colon cancer surgeries or the triple bypass; the diabetes, sleep apnea, or even the diagnoses of multiple sclerosis, some twelve years prior to landing ALS. I'd always figured my father's laundry list of health issues over the past decade or so would have meant he'd finally die of something completely unrelated, such as a meteor, or sinkhole. But he showed me, I suppose. My father, able to spend his final months at home, as he had requested, albeit with enormous assistance. Over his final weeks, nurses and personal care workers more likely to be wearing masks, to be repeatedly washing their hands. My father, unchanged.

Seven days after my father died, Anne Thériault's article "Some Deaths Are Lonelier Than Others" appeared online at *Flare*. "The coronavirus has taken away our ability to grieve collectively, forcing us to find new ways to mourn," she writes.

Not having that map right now is a bitter loss. Part of what people are struggling with is the fact that, in the middle of all this death, it feels like the script for how we navigate it has been taken away. What do you do when someone dies and you can't perform the usual rites, which for many have the added complication of also being religiously significant? How do you honour someone's life right now in a way that feels worthy of them? In what ways can we make individual deaths feel meaningful when they're just one among so many other deaths?

The week or two that followed, set in a fog. I spend three days crafting an obituary for my father, in part to centre myself, to make solid what otherwise felt like smoke. I needed something to be able to hold, to later be able to set down, when ready. When my mother died a decade earlier, I was unable, in the immediate, to write or say much at all, but the rituals were still in place. Had the world been normal, we would have had visitations on Tuesday evening and Wednesday morning, with a funeral immediately following at the church in the village. Instead, we schedule a Thursday service, to allow time for a Monday announcement by the province to see if any of the guidelines might be lifted. To allow ourselves time. It was all we had left.

On May 8, someone on Twitter asks: Why is it snowing? The following day, the same question. Today is colder than yesterday. The sky is overcast, and there's even some rain.

After my father's funeral, I attempt to return to the headspace of writing. This new post-father space. Given the three days I spent composing his obituary—between his death and the service—I've had to replace my background music from Brian Eno's ongoingness to Chopin's *Complete Nocturnes*, as performed by Brigitte Engerer. Eno had become infected with that onset of grief, an environment within which I did not wish to live. I required a turn of the page. Chopin, for now. Until a further page reveals itself.

I feel emotionally exhausted and attempt to figure out exactly what to do next. As Nathan Hill writes in his May "Postcard from the Pandemic: A Solid Little Feeling" for *Poets & Writers*: "It's a paradox: I've never had so much time to be productive, yet so little will to produce." If this suite of essays began as a deep dive into my distraction around global pandemic, another distraction has layered on top of another. I attempt to begin. I attempt some kind of spark or pilot light. As Ali Smith wrote, in *Artful* (2013):

> In the beginning was the word, and the word was what made
> the difference between form and formlessness, which isn't to
> suggest that the relationship between form and formlessness
> isn't a kind of dialogue too, or that formlessness had no words,
> just to suggest that this particular word for some reason made
> a difference between them—one that started things.

I am seeking that spark, that word. Can't you smell oil? At my father's funeral service, his former hired man, Jack McCourt, mentioned my father had said this during a visit, just prior to lockdown. *Can't you smell oil?* Jack couldn't, and neither could the furnace man my father called in. There's nothing wrong here. Two weeks prior to my father's death, his furnace exploded out from under him, bursting black oil smoke throughout the farmhouse at 3:00 a.m. The furnace is set directly underneath his main-floor bedroom, underneath his hospital bed. How did the furnace explode out and not up? Bits of metal dug deep in the wooden stairs, but the cellar ceiling unaffected. And while everyone else panicked, he remained unshaken. You're making too much of this, he told my sister. Can't you just put me in the shed?

I don't have to think about days of the week anymore. My tracking, every second Friday to head to the farm for a weekend of caregiving, is gone. I can't track days. Christine offers that I could, possibly, start paying attention to Rose's homeschooling, and the various Aoife and Rose school-related Zoom meetings scheduled throughout each week. She's right, of course, but she misses the substance of my loss of schedule, and the feeling of being untethered in grief. My father, my final parent, and the loss of the last vestiges of the family home, the family farm.

In Sabrina Orah Mark's column for the *Paris Review*, "Fuck the Bread. The Bread Is Over." posted May 7, she writes:

I send my sons on a scavenger hunt because it's day fifty-eight of homeschooling, and I'm all out of ideas. I give them a checklist: a rock, soil, a berry, something soft, a red leaf, a brown leaf, something alive, something dead, an example of erosion, something that looks happy, a dead branch on a living tree. They come back with two canvas totes filled with nature. I can't pinpoint what this lesson is exactly. Something about identification and possession. Something about buying time. As I empty the bags and touch the moss, and the leaves, and the twigs, and the berries, and a robin-blue eggshell, I consider how much we depend on useless, arbitrary tasks to prove ourselves. I consider how much we depend on these tasks so we can say, at the very end, we succeeded.

Somewhere it is snowing—Toronto, Buffalo—but not enough that it sticks to the ground. I am working to write myself out a haze and back into pandemic. *You Can't Catch Death*, Ianthe Brautigan wrote, composing a memoir about her infamous father, Richard Brautigan—on his life and fame, their life together, his suicide, and how she managed to navigate everything since. Or, as Anik See offered in "Letter to a Friend (Whose Mother Is Dying)," the opening piece in her *Saudade: The Possibilities of Place* (2008): "At the very least, it would seem that some comfort might be found in ritual. It's the best thing I can send your way right now, other than good thoughts."

I sit at my desk and attempt to write. To paraphrase the late poet John Newlove: It is little, but little enough. It is ritual, enough.

Christine gives Rose a haircut. Her hair was constantly tangling, and we were getting tired of telling her to stop chewing on the ends. Repeated warnings. Our first haircut of lockdown. I've been cutting my own hair since the late 1980s, so none of this affects my own grooming. I grow out my chops.

Lord of the Flies suddenly begins to trend on Twitter, at the appearance of an article in the *Guardian* about a group of schoolboys shipwrecked on a deserted island for fifteen months in the 1960s. The story contradicts William Golding's pessimistic view of humanity in his 1954 novel, and instead relays the community-bonding of six schoolboys who made a pact not to argue during their accidental isolation. The boys understood that they were stronger together, and they held themselves up across the distance of fifteen months. They had long been considered lost, with funerals held and family and friends left to mourn. And yet they survived.

I still seek my copy of Alice Notley's essays, dismantling another corner of my office shelves, a further corner of our book-lined suburban house. While I am not empty-handed, I still haven't found what it is I'm looking for. If I ever do discover it, might this project collapse? Am I working and thinking myself so directly toward that book that to reach my destination would complete that final thought? From a recent package from Pedlar Press in Newfoundland, I find myself going through Stan Dragland's latest collection of essays, *The Difficult* (2020): "As ideas made manifest, they fall into the category of conceptual art. One might be inclined to say that conceptual art makes its appeal to reason, not emotion, but I think anything that generates a spark of insight ignites at least the sensation of pleasure."

•

Fifty-seven days into lockdown, articles begin to emerge that speak of endings. How might this pandemic end? They claim the ending is two-fold, two-sided: the end of the disease itself, or the social ending, when those on voluntary lockdown grow tired, move to re-emerge, and simply live with the consequences. There are examples of those attempting to live with the consequences of ignoring safety measures even as we speak, from corners of the United States, to British Columbia and Quebec here in Canada. A friend out west is called back as university bookstore staff, and schools are set to open throughout la belle province. What changed? A week earlier, Quebec was holding tighter than most, but now it's willing to release those strict measures for the sake of reopening the economy. How much is a human life worth? How much is a population worth? A week ago, as Andrew Nikiforuk wrote of the lockdown for *The Tyee*, in his article "We Are in a New Danger Zone," fears of an economic depression and general fear for the future:

> We want this emergency to end. And many want it to end at any cost.
>
> And that is where the dangers lie. For we now live in the domain of a novel coronavirus.

Writing in early May for the CBC website on the unending lockdown and cold-weather records in Windsor, Casey Plett states: "In a long winter, my body can enter an amnesiac stasis. I forget the world can be another way." Articles speak of "murder hornets" entering the United States, a trickle that, unless stopped, could so easily become a wave.

Two further articles float by my Twitter feed: "Demand for P.E.I. School Food Program Is 4 Times Higher than When Pandemic Started" and "This Energy Analyst Says the Oil Sands Are 'Done'": "COVID-19 is making many bearish about bitumen. Deborah Lawrence's past pessimism has proven unpopular, and correct."

We are living through a space that is both the endless present and the impossible future. Will this be our new normal, with lockdowns, wearing face masks while shopping or at work, or might this be something we barely recall in five—or even two—years? Does anyone remember SARS, or H1N1? Will there be long-term effects of this global pandemic in how we interact with each other, or in the multiple social and income disparities being spotlit during this crisis? The Spanish flu altered the ways our public spaces were built, and changes we aren't even aware of anymore. On April 30, on the World Economic Forum website, Kate Whiting's interview with science journalist Laura Spinney spoke of that earlier pandemic, and the cultural effects that emerged in response; of those with lower immune systems struck first by the Spanish Flu, and the resulting baby boom of the 1920s from a population of young and healthy survivors. She spoke of the lower rates of literacy, which prompted rumours and misinformation to run rampant. Also, as Spinney offers:

> It gave a big boost to the concept of socialized medicine and healthcare, which no country had really got around to organizing yet. The pandemic is what gave the stimulus to do that because there was a realization that a pandemic was a global health crisis you had to treat at the population level. You couldn't treat individuals and there was no point in blaming individuals for catching an illness or treating them in isolation.
>
> What will Covid-19 bring? Could all of those meetings really have been emails?

Nova Scotia theatre director and playwright Ken Schwartz writes as part of his "Pandemic Diary" entry on the CBC website, "Today, I feel like a cobbler in a world of people who no longer wear shoes."

Once we wrestle the girls from their morning tablets, Rose and Aoife work to dismantle the living room and set up a substantial fort of all the blankets and pillows from their beds. By mid-morning, they insist I experience their structure from within. The inside of their fort is very dark. Even my voice seems muffled. Cool and quiet, it is all I can do to remain awake. Later on, a package of ordered materials arrives with the doorbell, and, as I open to see what it is, Aoife breaks down in tears, deeply upset that it wasn't her Oma. She misses her Oma and wants to see her. I don't know what to tell her.

•

Today I was pleased to see a new pandemic essay on the CBC website composed by my friend Gary Barwin, the award-winning Hamilton fiction writer, poet, and performer. His piece was delightful:

> Another morning, because I couldn't help myself, I wondered about the virus's perspective. What are its goals? What does it think of humans? Does it feel happy, sad, conflicted, guilty, hungry or misunderstood? Does it think of itself like a super-hero villain, trying to take over the world...or something else? What would its sense of community be like? And community with what? With other viruses?
>
> Last week, I wondered what if trees kept their distance, but were connected by a root system. Oh yeah. They are. "There's no place like rhizome. There's no place like rhizome."

Early in lockdown, Christine collected our wedding rings and set them aside. This will make handwashing easier, she said. I'm aware of this absence whenever I go for a walk, even if just to drop another handful of letters and postcards into the postbox around the corner. My left thumb seeks out what it knows is not there. It makes me aware of just how often I'd reached for it.

There are still cars on our street, and still buses that pass; still buses that, occasionally, even have passengers riding in them. We might not all be in the same boat, but we're all in the same storm. My mother-in-law apparently goes for walks with a friend, albeit at the required safe distance. They keep the length of an alligator between them. Or, as Conan O'Brien suggested: three Kevin Harts. Through all of these distances, might we see a resurgence of drive-in theatres? Multiple articles seem to think so. Years ago, at a reading in Montreal, I met comedian

Lorne Elliott, who casually mentioned he knew of my corner of Eastern Ontario due to the drive-in theatre that once sat just by Alexandria, where he and some friends spent much of their teen years, driving across the provincial border from Montreal. As he informed me: Did you know there weren't any drive-in theatres in Quebec?

From San Jose, California, footage emerges of dozens of goats roaming the streets. They move as a single wave, akin to Centretown sparrows circling a Bronson Avenue apartment tower.

Over in Denver, Colorado, apparently, my letter has finally reached Julie Carr, after a month in the mail. She responds via email with two poems, including "The Underscore," composed for New York City dancer and dance teacher Nancy Stark Smith. When I look up Smith's name, I discover she died the same day as my father, although far younger than he. Carr ends her short poem:

In this way we serve one another
with airdropped grasses in our phones

    Who is missing today? Who turned her camera off?
    Whose plane grazed the low cloud to release the rain

    that floods the back of my mirror again?

●

The Province of Ontario extends its state of emergency through to June 2. Where might we be by then? That's only two-and-a-half weeks ahead of us, which isn't that far. Los Angeles County is extending its stay-at-home orders a further three months. The *Chicago Sun-Times* offers an editorial against the push to reopen states, writing, "If the United States were to throw open the economy and bet on creating herd immunity without a vaccine, the death toll could run into the hundreds of thousands." Simultaneously, in Ottawa, the bulk of reported Covid-19 cases are "resolved," a word that includes both recovery and death. Ottawa Public Health reports that 70 per cent of 1,692 cases fall into that category, with 178 of those having resulted in death.

At some point soon, we aim to assist my sister with sorting through our father's house. What had once been ours. All this loss and this death and resulting shifts begin to collide.

It is somehow easier these days to get caught up in what previously wouldn't have been such a distraction, in the before-times. I see someone retweet something by David Cassidy, and I think, didn't he die? I float through Wikipedia pages and realize that, no, I was thinking of his half-brother Shaun Cassidy, but spend twenty minutes moving through both of their Wiki entries. Did you know that David Cassidy fathered nine children over the years with three different partners? The first of his children was born in 1981, and the most recent, 2011. That's a thirty-year gap, in case you were wondering. Boy, that's a lot.

I write a letter, I write a letter, I write another letter. Who am I missing? A designated mound of stamps and envelopes, and the walk around the corner into the postbox. I amuse myself by mailing out an array of 1970s-era poetry postcards by David W. McFadden, Geoffrey Young, Margaret Atwood, and George Bowering, produced as part of a special postcard issue of Ken Norris and Jim Mele's poetry journal,

CrossCountry. "In the olden days," I write, "people used to mail each other 'postal-cards' such as these. Can you imagine? It's like a tweet on paper!" I don't have that many left, despite the box Ken Norris passed along out of his basement storage, right before the reading we did together at the University of Maine back in November 2001. I've mailed out a dozen so far, with each one, at least to me, funnier than the last. Later this afternoon, I'll most likely walk with Aoife to the mailbox, once Christine begins setting up Rose's Zoom meeting for school, but that's still a couple of hours away. I spend twenty minutes on a "Penguin Classics Cover Generator," building a cover for the potential book this might be. Is that too optimistic? I pick up the idea via Facebook from Ottawa poet Amanda Earl, who caught it on Toronto poet Jacqueline Valencia's page. The process allows you to include a photograph as the top 60 per cent of the front cover, above the "Penguin Classics" logo, and include your name and book title in the black space beneath. Valencia's is a photograph of her clearly unimpressed cat, with the accompanying title *Fuck This Place.* My favourite-to-date has to be Gary Barwin, featuring a photograph of Sigmund Freud and his mother he'd posted for Mother's Day, only a day or two prior, alongside the title *Mama has armpits like umbrellas and Daddy won't come in out of the rain.* It's a very Barwinesque title, and some part of me now wishes to read this imaginary book. The process reminded Barwin that he'd actually made his own mock cover for his then-novel-in-progress *Yiddish for Pirates* (2016) in the classic Penguin orange-covered design, as a way to prompt him to continue writing. To make it real, so that he might finish it. Might this be what I'm doing as well?

I stroke my award-winning beard, attempting to seem thoughtful. Marion Poschmann's *The Pine Island* (2020) notes, as translated by Jen Calleja:

On the face of it, the matter of beards was quite straightforward. God had a full beard, Satan had a goatee. The latter could, iconographically speaking, be seamlessly traced back to the ancient depictions of the goat-bearded, goat-hooved, and goat-tailed Pan, and even today visual media, especially feature films, fall back on the beard when they need to flag up an undeniably morally reprehensible character. And the younger generation, once they hit puberty, naturally liked to flirt with the bad-guy image. Give themselves a mark of toughness in opposition to the rebuke that they're sissies. A younger generation with no prospects can't help but style themselves in a way that suggests that they are a force to be reckoned with.

Rose leads her sister in an endless loop of "Jingle Bells," or, at least, what little she knows of it. They sing for ten minutes before they lose interest and make their way into our sunroom, knocking over a series of empties.

There is a plastic eye on the floor of my office. It stares up at me.

•

Someone tweets a report of a brawl breaking out at an East York, Pennsylvania, Red Lobster, due to the three-hour wait times. People are this close, someone else responds, to losing it. My mother-in-law forwards us an article from CTV News, as Ontario-based owners of cottages in rural Quebec are voicing their frustrations, unable to visit or even check in on their properties. It is suggested that local residents in the area are reporting cars with Ontario plates to the police. What choice do they have? Out-of-towners entering a rural community and potentially utilizing what little medical resources such an outpost might hold, if they were to develop symptoms. And as Christine reminds me, Montreal is still considered a hot spot. The numbers out of Quebec are higher than those of the rest of the country.

As Charles Legere writes in the poem "The Coppices of Pleasure," in the latest issue of *FENCE magazine* (36 Winter Early 2020): "I can't recall the sensation of pleasure, only the context, which I would have to tell as a story."

I am thinking about time, and how one can't help but comprehend this temporal stretch as a formless mass. In her memorable *Elizabeth Smart: A Fugue Essay on Women and Creativity* (2004), Toronto writer Kim Echlin offers:

My own memory of giving birth is of how time and space disappeared at the end of my labor. I was the still centre; there was nothing but pain and breath. The threshold between life and death receded. The helping voices and tending hands around me seemed disembodied and remote. Through my own body I was both instrument and agent of nature. It is clear to me why certain women want to have many babies and why many women take new direction after childbirth.

Christine returns from an errand later than I had expected, having accidentally spent half an hour on the phone with our friend Shannon, who is home with twin boys born four pounds each some two or three weeks ago. They are all fine, by the way, despite the quarantine birth. Christine hums at the excitement of meeting them, although we have no idea when it might happen.

I discover, slipped inside as a folded bookmark in my copy of Echlin's book-length essay, the printout of an email I received from Vermont poet Paige Ackerson-Kiely, along with a poem she attached, "Love Poem to a Stranger." "I spied eleven lank deer in one evening," her poem begins, "feeding on different lots." The email is dated January 7, 2008, which seems an entire lifetime away from here, from now. Curious as to where the piece may have ended up, I eventually locate the published version of her poem, nearly intact but for some minor tweaking. She retitled the poem "Misery Trail," and it lives in her second full-length collection, *My Love Is a Dead Arctic Explorer* (2012). Hindsight suggests there is something of a placeholder aspect to the earlier title, but still, I wonder: how does one move so far, from the suggestion of a more wistful longing into something darker, over the span of some four years? Both versions of the fourteen-line poem end with the couplet

So I walked, uncharacteristically slow.
You couldn't know how slow I walked.

There. So there is such a thing as time.

It has been two months since our lockdown began, and the day of our last non-household social encounter. The day prior to my fiftieth birthday, when my birth mother came by to meet for the first time. Was that only then? If we don't mark these milestones, the days might just disappear. This one is different, and the next one will also be different. Can't you tell? Continuing to slowly drift through my bookshelves, I find myself rereading the late American poet Kathleen Fraser, from her *Discrete Categories Forced into Coupling* (2004):

> how a gesture intended as an opening can turn everything in another direction ruining (without having any idea why) an entire history between two persons at one time existing in relation, yet in this moment the discovery coming over one, unprepared for it—sudden piling of dark clouds in the corner of sky, south end of piazza, sun's light taken from any person sitting with face turned—how, years later, the impulse arrives similarly to hide or dip below the window, not to be seen

Christine mentions a mutual friend on Facebook who reports having to block someone else for their repeated posts citing conspiracy theories on Covid-19, the global pandemic, and the subsequent lockdown. She knows who it is, as do I. I try not to think too hard on it. The very idea exhausts.

Rose wears her elf pyjamas today. She and Aoife decided at bedtime last night to pull out their Christmas pyjamas. Once I convinced them off tablets this morning, she ran into my office and declared "I'm an elf!" before requesting a roll of tape so they can build paper candy canes. They are self-regulating their crafts, and have been for some time. Two rolls of tape later, they're handing out rolled-up construction paper as their candy canes, before moving on to their next project. They are very pleased.

As part of yardwork, I trip up our front steps, unable to see precisely where each step lands. I was to have cataract surgery scheduled for my right eye a few months back, with my left eye to follow close behind. I can see less through my right eye now than I could even a month ago, and I can feel my left eye going as well. I suspect this is also a factor in breaking a toe earlier in the year. If it gets much worse, I'll be unable to drive. Where is this going? All non-essential surgeries, they said.

Happy birthday, Bernadette Mayer. The much-beloved American poet turned seventy-five years old on May 12. How does one celebrate during a crisis? On our evening couch in the basement, I hear Christine repeat German words into her cellphone. She is taking an online language course, to attempt to reclaim what her mother's generation had, for the most part, set aside.

The National Capital Commission opens more of Ottawa's extensive parkway system to foot traffic during weekends, to offset the difficulties of social distancing. Why drive when you can walk?

I hear someone describe this period of time as a "collective trauma."

Did it rain yesterday, or did I imagine that? Or was that the day before? Today, I wake before Christine and allow her the rare space of sleeping in. By the time she rouses, coffee. The children are downstairs, post-tablets, happily fed.

When I "discovered" the work of American poet Cassie Donish through their stunning second collection, *The Year of the Femme* (2019), I spent a few minutes cursing Slope Editions under my breath for not sending a copy of Donish's debut, *Beautyberry* (2018), immediately upon publication. Later on, I realize this book is already on my poetry shelves. It was filed, of course, under "d." For all my complaining, I thought, the least I could do would be to read it. *Beautyberry* offers:

under the surfaces
were more surfaces

US poet Tom Snarsky posts an image of Jean Valentine's poem "He Disappeared into Complete Silence": "But called back, through / the closed-off wooden ceiling, to his / speech returned." Elsewhere on Twitter, I catch an article that speaks to a rise in reported hate crimes in Vancouver, and how the BC government rents out a hotel in Victoria to temporarily house some of the homeless population.

Montreal writer Jacob Wren opens his *Rich and Poor* (2016) with:

There is the expression: you catch more flies with honey than
you do with poison. But I have realized this is only partly true.
Because unless your goal is to breed flies, you also need at least
a little bit of poison to finish them off. Looking back on my life
I now wonder: what was the honey and what was the poison?

I've long considered Wren an underappreciated writer, despite the many books he's published over the years, edging his meditative prose up against theory and philosophy far closer to European models of literary writing than most of his Canadian contemporaries. I thought this, too, back during his Toronto days, when he published poetry titles under the moniker "Death Waits." How many names, you might ask, has he gone through? The past, and even the present, can be remarkably fluid, one might say, as can identity. He repeatedly writes his way into being. Isn't this the same thing I said about Nicole Brossard? Perhaps it is the very nature of Montreal. And yet, even a hot spot in Montreal is unable to rewrite itself by reopening schools.

I'll admit I begin to feel a bit squirrelly from the repeating days, but perhaps this is all luxury also. I am not required to leave the house, but for the weekends I once left for the homestead to care for my dying father. I no longer leave the house. Perhaps this is luxury, but perhaps, too, this is grief. I feel an inch away from Michael Douglas's character in *Wonder Boys* (2000), standing outside in track pants, slippers, and pink robe. "I am working on my book," I tell myself. I've already been driving to pickup errands wearing my slippers, which Christine keeps telling me not to do. Slippers salvaged from my late father's belongings, I might add. I open the trunk of the car from the driver's seat, and a teenager fills the car with grocery bags. How privileged is this? I walk the five steps from parked car to postbox in my slippers, and push letters through the slot, working on faith alone that any of these might be delivered within a reasonable timeline. But then, Christine offers of the *Wonder Boys* comparison—to truly complete the look, I would need to move away from my daily addiction to what she calls "hard pants."

The only part of the upcoming millennium he dreaded, said 1990s icon Fox Mulder in an episode of *X-Files*, was the return of drawstring pants.

There are some lines, still, that I shall never cross.

Prompted by a conversation over email with Montreal poet émilie kneifel, I'm again working my way through *Crosscut Universe: Writing on Writing from France* (2000), a book edited and translated by Norma Cole. Vancouver poet Michael Turner had responded positively to some work I'd published of kneifel's, posting on his blog: "A lot of poems these days as lineless blocks and those with lines that break for no reason, as if their authors take their cues from pictures, which is fine, we're a visual culture." I found his comments curious, although admittedly there are many who work the shape of prose poems without really understanding the form. Turner himself certainly seems to know what he's doing. Over email, kneifel responded to Turner's prompt:

> would love to chat with you about this more, whenever. his comment about blocks just being visual/ not having a reason. my prose poetry feels very intentional; i've never been drawn to the meaning making of enjambment in my own work; i find i need the density of a prose poem in order to get any traction towards the feeling i am trying so hard to scramble after.

The shape of the prose line, and the poetic form, has so much to do with the final piece. How does one write in a crisis? Most of the work I find most striking in the collection, and return to most often, are the prose poems by French poet Emmanuel Hocquard, writing on form as the shape of thought as much as a shape of writing or language. As the piece "Fragment" begins: "The *fragment* deserves our attention for a moment, if only by virtue of the fact that for some it causes a technical discomfort." I have been here long enough that I have begun to repeat myself. The following piece in the collection is his "How," a prose poem speaking directly to a further element of poetic structure:

To write an elegy, you have to know how an elegy is made. And to find out how an elegy is made, treat it just like an engine. Choose a standard elegy, take it apart and study the separate pieces lying on the table.

This seems very Victorian, the idea of understanding something through dismantling it. A pocket watch, for example. I approach my writing through entirely opposite means, attempting to comprehend a form through construction. I build, and I build, writing my slow way into making sense of and through form, structure, and meaning. There was a theory during the era of the Industrial Revolution that described God as a watchmaker, adding: "what watchmaker only makes one watch?" Every era and culture has its notion of divine creator, after all. Most of these assessments offering little more than a reflection back. A pocket watch or a dead frog. You might dismantle a watch to try to understand it, but grade schoolers doing the same in their science classes were left with little more than a dead frog. Try to put *that* back together.

"It's impossible to fail if one doesn't know how the end should look," writes American writer Sarah Mansguso in her *300 Arguments* (2017). "And it's impossible to succeed. But it's possible to enjoy." I catch a freshly posted article on *Lit Reactor* that speaks to writing while parenting small children, especially during the lockdowns. The entire article boils down to "write when you can," with the appropriate amount of "don't feel guilty" sprinkled in. This is what I did when our girls were smaller; I wrote in bursts as toddler Rose napped, fully aware that once she woke, my writing day would end. It is important to be realistic about one's goals, after all, and the difficulties in attempting them. Some days, those windows to work were less than ninety minutes. I am still seeking that collection of essays by Alice Notley, which might have become my white whale. I've somehow decided that this writing requires it but might also not be able to survive beyond it. What am I searching for? Perhaps I should spend more of my time on the blank page, as Robert Kroetsch suggested in *A Likely Story: The Writing Life* (1995):

> A scrapbook is an exceptional kind of book in that it comes to us as a collection of blank pages. We must become authors before we can become readers. Or perhaps we must become readers before we can become authors.
>
> Right there is a lesson that first-year students struggle to learn. Perhaps instead of giving each new student a giant heap of books to read, we should present each with a blank book and invite him or her to fill it with the story of how one gets an education.

On May 16, the *New York Times* wrote of former American president Barack Obama delivering a virtual commencement speech, "urging thousands of graduates at historically black colleges and universities 'to seize the initiative' at a time when he says the nation's leaders have fumbled the response to the coronavirus pandemic." Addressed to "more than 27,000 students at 78 participating historically black colleges and universities," the commencement speech was one of the rare addresses he's given in such a public sphere since the end of his presidency. With the absence of leadership in the current White House during this crisis, Obama's address was both direct and optimistic, speaking to a wider American populace on the disparities that have come to light throughout the pandemic, and how any community is stronger together than apart, asking for calm, fortitude, and a resolve to work together.

"Whether you realize it or not, you've got more road maps, more role models, and more resources than the Civil Rights generation did," he said. "You've got more tools, technology, and talents than my generation did. No generation has been better positioned to be warriors for justice and remake the world."

Even the blank page is _______ .

The mind seeks out patterns, even where none might exist.

Around midnight, a skunk bombs the house. The smell permeates the main floor, although our bedroom window is open, so perhaps we've some options to air out the space. We'd had it happen before, a few years earlier, but the cold weather prevented us from airing the house out as quickly and easily, and the 4:00 a.m. barrage woke everyone. By morning, we can barely tell the pre-midnight burst occurred. The children don't seem to have noticed.

Seeking out another title, I locate the copies of those lost Anansi books, underneath a stack of mail. John Elizabeth Stintzi's *Junebat* (2020), the first poem of which opens: "As summer inches onward and my life empties out." How easily this sentence applies to our two-plus months of lockdown. And yet we are safe. We are safe but stir-crazy, wondering about the uncertainties of what might come next.

Toronto streets begin to close to vehicle traffic, which prompts a significant increase in pedestrians and cyclists. Everyone keeps their distance. The long weekend is warm, sunny, and significant. A long weekend that lasts seemingly forever, although there are reports of Ontario businesses that might be able to open, come Tuesday. And on Tuesday, as well, an update on preschools, daycares, and schools. I've already heard the suggestion that schools might begin, once they do, at one day a week. What might that look like for what students have lost? Would this extend the whole summer and into the fall, as some kind of continuous school year?

At the beginning of May, my brother-in-law, Corey, returned to work. He works in construction, unable to deflect away from being called essential. If it doesn't meet its contract deadline for completion, he says, his company sets itself up to be sued. At least, that is the way I understand it.

Kyle Dodson—@KyleDodsonFunny—tweets: "hey seniors, if you're really missing graduation sit in the sun wearing a shower curtain while someone reads from a phonebook for 3 hours."

•

Apparently it is Victoria Day in Canada, and Christine and the young ladies have spent much of the day in the backyard. They requested I turn on the tap in the basement, so they could use the hose to water the garden and fill up their water table. By mid-afternoon, Christine fried up some dandelion heads with batter, a dish known as "fritters." Rose serves me a small bowl in my office: four still-warm fritters, coated in maple syrup. What's this? We're living in a pandemic, Christine responds, and we need to learn how to live off the land. Before I'm able to sample them, I'm forced to spend twenty minutes or so pulling multiple Smarties out of Aoife's doll's mouth. Why are there Smarties stuck in the doll's mouth?

"In literature," Devin Johnston wrote, as part of his *Creaturely and Other Essays* (2009), "smell and taste often stand in for the mute fact of lived experience." He continues:

> Though I cannot verify the claim, I suspect that the chemical senses can be found most often in works of autobiography or memoir. Marcel Proust, after all, wrote thousands of pages on the flavor of a petit madeleine soaking in tea and what memories it evokes. The taste and its associations are inextricable yet ultimately uncommunicable.

Perhaps I am doing my job properly, after all, or at least possibly, according to Johnston. Once the doll's mouth was cleared. The taste of the fritters corresponded to dandelion heads coated in batter, with a layer of real maple syrup. I have known of cooking with dandelions for some time, and have been curious about it, including the possibility of dandelion wine. Thank you for that, Ray Bradbury.

I ate the fritters, but I was not convinced.

An article in *Marie Claire* offers that the coronavirus lockdowns might force Queen Elizabeth II to retire permanently from her royal duties, which are on hold until the fall, at least. It has already been noted that her announcements are now followed immediately and similarly by announcements by Prince Charles, to remind the Commonwealth, it would seem, that he is, indeed, King-in-Waiting. Kayleigh Roberts quotes royal biographer Andrew Motion:

> "Prince Charles is, of course, over 70 himself but he has had the virus and probably has immunity now," Morton explained, adding that he still sees the Queen as playing a public role, even if it's in a virtual capacity. "We will have a Zoom monarchy, she will be Her Majesty the screen."

The world changes in incremental ways, and in ways we don't easily and can't yet understand. It changes in ways we might not return from, an idea with both positives and negatives. The Queen is ninety-four years old, after all. This is the weekend named after her great-great-grandmother. Known as the unofficial onset of the Canadian summer, or May-two-four weekend, it is also celebrated as the official birthday of the late British monarch. Another birthday under lockdown. According to Wikipedia, the Parliament of the Province of Canada officially designated May 24 as the Queen's birthday back in 1845, and Victoria herself was born that day back in 1819. Today is Victoria Day, despite May 24 actually being seven further days ahead of where we currently are. Is it any wonder we lose track of time? The day is designated by fireworks, parades, and picnics, and I suppose dandelion heads might be the closest we come this year, although I have yet to leave the house at all today, even for the sake of the backyard. Perhaps it would be better if the holiday might be shifted away from such settler considerations, moving into something to acknowledge the original inhabitants of what the Crown came to pilfer.

Christine returns again from the yard with a fresh assortment of dandelions. These, she says with a sparkle in her eye, picking the heads apart and collecting them in a measuring cup, will be made into shortbread.

●

I write because I am able to. Because it is how I respond to the world. Because I am paying attention to these briefings and changes and details and wish not to be overcome by them, wish not to be rendered immobile. If I couldn't work due to distraction, I thought, why not make the distraction itself the work? And now here I am, nearly two months down the line, sketching out notes from the inside, of both house and global pandemic. *If you discover these notes*, I might have said at one point, *remember me.*

I hear Texas has reopened, and subsequently reports its largest number of daily new cases. Mary Oliver, writing on poetry in *A Poetry Handbook: A Prose Guide to Understanding and Writing Poetry* (1994): "Whatever can't be taught, there is a great deal that can, and must, be learned." Just how might you approach the current state of the world, Mary Oliver?

One thing we have learned during lockdown: Aoife is very good at pretend baby-crying. She uses it often, as part of the girls' games. There are times either Christine or I feel one of us must get up and check, just to make sure. No, they say, this is part of our game.

I'm behind on everything, only now opening up the pages of a new poem that Stephen Brockwell emailed for me to read back in April. He writes:

> I said, I refuse to believe in something
> that can't be said.

> That seems about right.

In the before-times, Monday was my housecleaning day. With more time at my desk through the weekend, by Monday afternoon, after collecting Aoife from preschool, I would start in on the house, attempting to recruit her into service, of course. Vacuuming and washing floors, putting away dishes. Picking up all the toys, a task I've been pushing for the young ladies to participate in far more often. They are old enough, after all. Laundry is constant—some two loads every three days—although vastly improved in our household since our years of cloth diapers. And yet, there is always, somehow, laundry.

Mondays no longer have the same post-weekend push. What are days? What are weekends? Our floors require cleaning more often, and toys are scattered across them with more regularity. I discover a pair of scissors on the young ladies' bedroom floor, and paper scraps. A drawing they've taped to their bedroom door. I am more often cleaning; I am more often reminding them to pick up. Why is there a towel on the floor? Why is that wrapper there? Why is a slice of half-eaten bread under that chair?

Lately I've noticed more joggers passing the house.

Ontario announces schools won't reopen until September, at the earliest. We are relieved, having discussed this last night. Had they already opened one day a week, might we have sent Rose in at all? Aoife is scheduled for junior kindergarten this fall, which Christine reminds me is not mandatory. We could keep her home.

Christine works on our garden. She pre-orders meat and vegetables from an array of local vendors, aware of the potentials for shortage. Large bags of dirt and mulch appear in our driveway.

●

There have been reports on fatigue—the two months-plus of lock-down, and the exhaustion that inevitably follows. How does one exist in a pandemic? I'm sitting at my desk with my first cup of morning coffee to read from Buffalo, New York, poet Noah Falck's latest, *Exclusions* (2020):

The entire world is room temperature.
Sunlight bleeds over the city,
and the mallwalkers gather
to form a sort of nervous system
or fatigue performance, we say.

I can hear Christine and Aoife in the bedroom, singing. The sun is warm and the girls spend their days in our backyard wading pool or leaping through the sprinkler, but we're still waking up later than we should.

It is reported that Annie Glenn, widow of US astronaut John Glenn, has died at one hundred, due to Covid-19-related illness. Teju Cole, in the *New York Times Magazine*: "History's first draft is almost always wrong—but we still have to try and write it." There is only so much one can see from the inside. He states updated numbers and further updated numbers and asks, where is the grief? Everywhere, it would seem, writers and journalists are coming out of the woodwork, all attempting to comprehend what, for now, might still be too impossibly large to understand. Through all of this there is still poverty, still food shortages, still factors such as floods, fires, and tornadoes that refuse to stand still. There is racism, and obscene amounts of income disparity. "I keep thinking about floods," Cole writes, "and how only after the waters recede do the bodies of the drowned become visible." By the time you are reading this, what might we have seen?

Letters arrive, from Amanda Earl and Pearl Pirie, responding to mine. Pearl's letter also includes a poem on fatigue. She writes:

fatigue
from sustained concentration

a focus I thought I could never regain / but did [...]

I bet if the trees were text
I'd find them and their leaf galls illegible

Pearl and her husband, Brian, live in rural Quebec, where they've built a small house on a parcel of land, so isolation takes on new meaning from where they've settled. Through all of this, they still have their same trees, the same squirrels, the same spring growth.

Christine informs me that our particular Ottawa ward is now considered a "hot spot," second only to Rideau. Numbers don't lie, I suppose, but increased testing might shift them as well. We do not leave the house. We wash our hands. We wash our hands.

●

Global pandemic has me thinking differently about connection. Since lockdown began, I've composed and mailed over one hundred letters. Who have I missed? Who haven't I heard from? I think of certain friends and acquaintances living alone, or some I've seen shift in mood in their online presences. I work to reach out, touch base. How are you, really. In April, my *Touch the Donkey* mailout was twice as large as it might normally have been. I've been mailing out books to those I think might appreciate them, and postcards, and handfuls of brightly coloured literary ephemera. In my mind, this is precisely the time we should be reaching out to connect, and a physical piece of mail might be far more appreciated over these days. The mail might be slower, but it is mail, nonetheless. Everything seems slowed down to a crawl. I used to send email, and now I walk the two blocks to the postbox and shove envelopes in. Arrival might just take weeks.

In her *Concordance* (2020), Susan Howe offers: "Echo echo I love you. Breathe breathe."

Ashley C. Ford tweets: "You are watching people go through withdrawal from the emotional addiction to the myth of certainty."

Last night we watched the BBC documentary *Britain's Real Monarch* (2004), hosted by Tony Robinson, formerly of perennial favourites *Time Team* and *Black Adder*. The hour-long film traced a lineage from details that had emerged basically confirming that Edward IV was illegitimate, as his father, Richard Plantagenet, had been roughly one hundred miles distant for the five-week stretch around when his wife, Cecily, Duchess of York, would have conceived. Moving through genealogical research, the doc seeks out who would have been heir to the throne if not Edward, and thusly, a lineage of Plantagenets down throughout England until, as Wikipedia specifies, "The 14th Earl of Loudoun (who usually styled himself simply as Michael Hastings), who had emigrated to Australia in 1960, married, fathered five children, and lived in Jerilderie, New South Wales..." Christine and I thought it interesting as an exercise, but also rather silly to see it through that far. At the end of his forty-minute excursion, Robinson turned to the camera and asked, why are we going through this? He offered how tenuous this is, was, and could have been, with several examples of how this one particular line might have prospered differently. How seemingly random, with but one event here or there turning the fortunes of generations in an entirely different direction. There is no divine right of kings.

Craig Santos Perez tweets out his "Coronavirus Dream Song 14," a piece subtitled *"mutating John Berryman"* that begins: "Quarantine, friends, is boring. We must not tweet so." Perhaps this is how the world responds to global pandemic, Covid-19, and seemingly eternal lockdowns: by simply adapting. Over at *Mother Jones*, a May 22 article by Delilah Friedler profiles Rebecca Solnit, who discusses how difficult it is to see large effects and change occurring from the inside, and how frightening that is for so many. Presuming, of course, they have the luxury of an attention span away from focusing on mere survival.

I'm constantly reminding people that we're in the middle of a fairy tale. We want to know how it ends, but we're not at the end, we're in the middle. And that's really hard. Being in the middle of a story is a really hard place for people. They want to skip ahead and see how it ends. And when it's history, you don't get to skip ahead. People who are really informed about pandemics can make guesses about what's going to happen. But nobody knows exactly. And wisdom and intelligence consists of knowing that you don't know.

Perez's "Coronavirus Dream Song 14" continues:

After all, the news tickers, the death toll tocks,
we ourselves tick and tok,
and moreover my mother told me as a boy
(naggingly) 'Ever to confess you're bored
means you have no

Internet connection.'

I like how Perez plays with John Berryman's poem, shifting his "inner resources" to "Internet connection," shifting the internal to the external, something that, also, has become as omnipresent, essential, and even lacking in some corners of the world as water, democracy, and health care. Over at the *Paris Review*, Jana Prikryl wrote on Berryman's poem in a short essay posted February 23, 2012:

In "Dream Song #14," the drama, or antidrama, is Henry's boredom, a thing that is especially tricky to convey. I never tire of the comic-grave, drooping yet metrically perfectionist, repetitious thespian roundelays of this poem. "Ever to confess

you're bored / means you have no // Inner Resources" is how
Henry quotes his scolding mother. It's a maxim both wearily
conceded and richly facetious. If the brunt of some of the best
lyric poetry is that we must strip the costumes off our feelings
and confess them truly, Henry is strewing his alternative pro-
paganda that—honestly? dishonestly?—he has none just now.
No gainful feelings. And the costumes are of greater interest.

Someone mentions that one difference between Canadians and
Americans is that the latter wear shoes in the house. Is this true? Why
would Americans wear shoes in the house?

•

As Americans celebrate Memorial Day in lockdown, more than a few on social media post Frank O'Hara's "Memorial Day 1950": "…but then / the war was over, those things had survived / and even when you're scared art is no dictionary."

The *New York Times* offers, as the May 24 front page of its Sunday edition, a full-page examination of names and obituaries of a fraction of the nearly 100,000 American deaths due to Covid-19. An accompanying article online speaks to the reasoning behind the decision: "'I wanted something that people would look back on in 100 years to understand the toll of what we're living through,' Mr. Lacey said in an email."

One hundred thousand deaths, and but a fraction of the worldwide toll. Still, the exhaustions continue, combined with warm summer weather. A park in Toronto sees an onslaught of activity, which sets the internet ablaze. Both the Toronto mayor and the Ontario premier react in horror: this can't be happening. Everyone is crowded too close. We don't wish for these lockdown measures to be in place any longer than they have to be. Why are you risking the possibility of someone else's health crisis? Pockets of similar gatherings appear in various corners of Canada and across the United States, alongside continued protests. *We want a haircut!* And then the follow-up reports of a hairdresser who potentially exposed more than fifty clients. Where does this end?

The Pope says you can worship at home and don't require an intercessor. Isn't that the opposite of what the Catholic Church has been arguing for centuries?

We have a power outage, just as I'm typing, although it lasts less than a minute. Just long enough to pause the Chopin nocturnes I'm still listening to via YouTube. Just long enough to knock out an array of digital clocks throughout the house. The children, out in the yard in their swimming suits, don't notice.

One element of continued lockdown I've appreciated is in seeing how well our two young ladies play together, making up games and stories and songs. We knew of this prior, but our appreciation deepens. Once we daily wrestled them off their tablets, our first couple of weeks included the television on in the basement, which quickly became background to their attentions. After a while, they stopped even bothering going downstairs at all, unless they were wrapped up in some complicated game involving forts or babies or Cinderella. How many times has our dining room table become centre stage for one of their structures, or the site of a self-determined Lego city, a mound of drawings or some other invention? Today, self-slathered in sunscreen, they navigate the hose and their wading pool out in the backyard, occupying themselves for hours. I grew up on a farm, so I very early on learned the benefit of managing my own time, wandering the fields, collecting stones. The last thing I want to do is micromanage the young ladies, although I do attempt to get Rose to draw daily in one of her notebooks and report on her drawing. We've only managed this once, but I keep trying. I check in on them regularly. Or they come inside, seeking freezies. Little wet footprints on the floor of my office that run down the hall.

Another element I've appreciated is the array of stories that have drifted up, out of the ether, of comparable stories from days gone past. This is not the first time in memory that those in the world have lived through such a situation, even if some of the details might be slightly different. Public television offers a small tale of a centenarian living through the current pandemic who was born during the lockdown of the Spanish flu, her mother somehow managing solo throughout birth and her newborn daughter's first few months. *You can do this*, the piece offers. *You can get through this.* In the June issue of *Smithsonian Magazine*,

Emily Moon's short article "How the U.S. Fought the 1957 Flu Pandemic" begins:

> In April 1957, a new strain of a lethal respiratory virus emerged in East Asia, caught local health authorities by surprise and eventually killed masses of people worldwide. Today, in the age of Covid-19, that scenario sounds frighteningly familiar—with one key difference. Maurice Hilleman, an American microbiologist then running influenza monitoring efforts at the Walter Reed Army Institute of Research, saw the problem coming and prepared the United States ahead of time. "This is the pandemic," he recalled saying. "It's here."

This is not historically abstract in the way the 1918 Spanish flu pandemic might appear to us, but rather something, for many people, that occurred within living memory. To remember the 1957 pandemic, one might say, would put you disproportionally right in the path of Covid-19. Back then, there was notice, notification, and response, and 116,000 Americans succumbed to the disease, although far more could have been killed. Over email, Bay Area poet Susanne Dyckman offers her own:

> When I was a baby I had scarlet fever, and the Chicago Board of Health tacked a quarantine notice on our basement apartment door. My mother's not alive (gone too early) but I so wish I could talk to her about it, how she managed with an infant and a five year old, even something as basic as how she got groceries. All she ever told me was that we, as a family, were under quarantine (of course, somehow my doing?). Later, still being a kid when she told me the story, I didn't think to ask questions. Now I'm beginning to see what it takes to manage.

According to family lore, my mother caught scarlet fever while babysitting, although I've no clue if there were any quarantines for her, still living at home with her parents and four of six siblings. It was this that, according to family lore, affected her health and began the eventual loss of her kidneys, and resulted in her inability to bear children. Isolated incidents are never that, and there are lessons to learn from any situation. And yet we can watch in real time as segments of the population refuse the lessons and warnings of history.

It is hard to look at those numbers and see, on the other side, individuals holding up handmade signs proclaiming "I want a haircut!" With fear comes desperation. And there is little logic to, or argument against, desperation. Someone on Twitter suggests that of course there are those who consider haircuts, the casino, and other short-term pleasures worth the risk. Because they've no hope for anything else.

•

I still haven't located that title by Alice Notley. From Catherine Taylor's *Apart* (2016):

> Like the sentence, the people move forward, want resolution, seek conclusions, note parallels, but they, of course reach no final revelations, no concluding periods—no time with an end, no discrete clause of history, no full stop.
>
> A period is an interval of time in a cyclic motion; a period is determined by recurring phenomena.
>
> (Listen.) Even a sentence can seem like a pendulum.

Having run out of superhero movies and our array of television series, Christine and I have begun to turn our attention to documentaries—a three-part documentary on England's King Charles I and another on Lady Jane Grey, the first female British monarch, if only for nine days. Why, Christine asks, rhetorically, through the process, do I always forget about Queen Anne? "It's difficult to get the news *from* poems," writes Cole Swensen in her *Noise That Stays Noise: Essays* (2011), "because it's difficult to get the news *into* poems. What role does poetic language, or poeticity itself, play in that difficulty?" I've barely attempted to compose a poem now in, what, three or four months? After such a length of time, the question I always ask myself is *will I even remember how?*

Lying down with Rose as part of bedtime, Christine reports that Rose asked: "Mama, did you ever wonder if we were just a part of your dream? That you've been dreaming for a hundred billion years, and me and Aoife are just part of your dream?"

On May 26, on *Marker*, Steve LeVine's article, "Our Economy Was Just Blasted Years into the Future," offers how the "crisis is compressing and accelerating trends that would have taken decades to play out."

We are already seeing the shifts. This particular post-pandemic world will be different, once we emerge, than it was before we entered.

Before the coronavirus, surveillance capitalism was already a big worry—Big Tech companies were vacuuming up data from laptops, front doors, appliances, kitchens, living rooms, and smartphones and selling the resulting market intelligence for hundreds of billions of dollars a year. Now, touchless technology suggests a new front in the age of around-the-clock commercialized surveillance, hackable by Iran, China, North Korea, Russia, or any number of private actors, well- or malignly intended. It is an unusual, once-in-a-lifetime, super-charging event for Clear and its surveillance rivals, rebranding themselves while becoming an answer for companies, offices, and agencies everywhere contemplating how to safely reopen.

A friend of a friend, Alex Moore, posts a placard to Facebook, which I see through it being forwarded: "Under the current Guidelines your Milkshake is only permitted to bring 4 boys to the yard, max."

●

"But to say that one is suspicious of absolutes," writes Siri Hustvedt, in the introduction to *A Woman Looking at Men Looking at Women: Essays on Art, Sex, and the Mind* (2016), "is not the same as saying, for example, that the laws of physics do not theoretically apply to everything." I am thinking about change and about progress, and about the straight line. I am thinking how not even a perfectly straight line is consistent, given it has still a beginning, a middle, and an end. Each element can't be mistaken for another. Even if we appear unchanged by the end of this period, we will remain changed. What intrigues me is how those changes might manifest, from the largest to the smallest. Who might we become?

I watch as more than a couple of friends via social media express frustration with their situations, whether the opportunity for quiet solitude, or the weariness of missing out on being able to meet up with friends or family. Some have birthdays they are unable to attend to; others, deaths. There is no simple solution. A few days ago, I was invited to participate in a birthday greeting for American poet Samuel Ace, asked to send in a video of no more than thirty seconds in length. I had our young ladies participate, fully aware of how excited they would be, yet again, to sing happy birthday. With no disrespect to Samuel Ace, a fine human being and remarkably gifted poet, I should point out that our young ladies would sing happy birthday just as easily and enthusiastically to a rock or a goat or a pencil sharpener, I'd wager, as to a stranger via video over the internet. The only variance is when Rose turns at the appropriate time to be reminded who it is she is singing for, so she can sing out their name. Happy birthday, dear... ("Samuel," I whisper) ... Samuel, happy birthday to you.

American writer John Pavlovitz's May 4 blog post, "I Think You May Be Wasting Freedom," responds directly to those of his fellow citizens who are protesting lockdown. It is hard to comprehend how anyone in North America would conflate a Black protester's anti-police violence sign "Stop Shooting Us" with a white protester's anti-lockdown slogan "I Want a Haircut," and Pavlovitz has clearly had enough. And why are so many of the signs by anti-lockdown protesters misspelled? Pavlovitz writes:

> You are interpreting your temporary and fleeting inconvenience as perpetual and inhumane persecution—that's how soft and sad we've become, how small our battles now are, what we see as worthy causes.

I am thinking about letters, and the number I've sent out into the world, and the few I've received in turn. I am thinking about the social media responses to my postcards, Stuart Ross and Alex Porco reacting with slightly confused delight at the poems that appeared in their mailboxes. Porco, specifically, who couldn't believe I had sent him a poem by William Bronk, one of his favourite poets. How did you know? he asked. I'd seen him post on Bronk some days earlier and decided that sending him a copy of the Bronk postcard I had on hand seemed most obvious.

Perhaps this, too, is an example of something that can only be seen from a distance.

There are three deaths during lockdown proclaimed as outright murders of innocent civilians, all Black civilians, by police: Breonna Taylor in Louisville and George Floyd in Minneapolis, and Regis Korchinski Paquet in Toronto, who was both Black and Indigenous. There is outrage. There are protests, riots, looting. A police officer's knee on George Floyd's neck for nine minutes as Floyd repeated that he couldn't breathe and finally stopped responding. Killed for something he didn't actually do, for something that would have resulted in a minor charge, even if he had done it. No one deserves death. In Minneapolis, the protests rage for three, four, five consecutive nights so far, with multiple fires set throughout the city, including at a police precinct. The president refers to the looters and protesters as thugs. If you are more outraged by the looting, someone tweets, than the murder, you need to check yourself. Several protesters are shot by police in Louisville. Everyone is on edge.

The killing will only stop when we admit why there is killing. When we admit to our collective failures. Only there can we finally begin. How does one write in a crisis?

I saw someone else write: We should not be writing further pages of Claudia Rankine's *Citizen: An American Lyric* (2014). And then, of course, there is M. NourbeSe Philip, from *Zong!* (2008):

was

    the weight in being

    the same in rains

    the ratio in loss

the proved in fact

the within in is

the sufficient in indictment

the might have in existed

is

the evidence in negroes

We sit at six days, eight days, eleven consecutive days of worldwide protest at police brutality against Black individuals and Black communities, sparked by the police murder of George Floyd on May 25 in Minneapolis. There has been so much grief, so much loss. So much anger. What is it about this death that has galvanized a movement? *Abolish the police. Defund the police.* John Oliver speaks of the historic establishment of police to keep Black communities down, to keep the slaves from escaping. To know their place. Ten consecutive days during which I am unable to write, unable to add anything to this sprawling manuscript. I am stunned, heartsore, grieving. To understand that I am part of the problem and I have benefitted from it. I try very much to listen. Conan O'Brien, Stephen Colbert, and Seth Meyers each bring on guests to speak of their experiences and add to the conversation. For a week on Seth Meyers, one of his writers, Amber Ruffin, who is a Black woman, opens the broadcast with a different daily story of her experiences with the police, some of which are quite frightening. There is so much I clearly do not understand, nor have I ever. Reggie Watts and James Corden break down in tears during a discussion on race and Watts's experiences growing up in the midwest. It is a powerful moment, and deeply uncomfortable for its intimacy, Watts's raw emotion.

There is no more space for simply not being racist. One has to be *anti*-racist. Proactive. Two years ago, discussing #IdleNoMore, and a relative responded, Why can't they just be happy to be Canadian? And how I actually shook, not knowing how exactly to respond. I tried to explain as best as I could, without resorting to anger or frustration. It made me aware of just how exhausting and infuriating this might be for Aboriginal peoples, forced to defend their own rights and humanity, ad nauseum. The realization that I have no idea.

I am reluctant to speak, wishing not to say the wrong thing. A stupid thing. Reluctant to speak, aware that mine isn't the voice anyone wishes to hear from. Is that, then, also a cop-out? It's almost enough to forget we're in the midst of a global pandemic. Fear of the pandemic is overtaken by rage, frustration, and resolve. Protests occur, but with face masks for protection. Concerns grow that these might evolve into new hot spots for Covid-19, but the protests continue. Certain police and politicians take a knee. The White House, as well as certain police higher-ups, somehow manage to make the situation worse, through press conferences, announcements, tweets. What the absolute hell is wrong with you?

Peaceful protesters worldwide gather against systemic racism and police violence, and the police respond with war gear, war tactics, attacking peaceful demonstrators and journalists alike, both on and off camera. Their response clarifies the issue: this is about power, and control. This was never about public safety. In many cities, the police react with brutal violence, aghast that anyone would dare question their tactics or motives, or suggest any kind of oversight. In this, they prove, as a collective, the value in defunding their efforts for the sake of community-based solutions. This can't go on.

Black Lives Matter takes over the newsfeed. There are moments one nearly forgets we're in the midst of a global pandemic. Footage of peaceful protests worldwide, hundreds of thousands of people marching in solidarity against police violence. Hundreds of thousands of people in face masks. Unfortunately, too, the too-frequent bits of footage of police bringing violence to peaceful protests, police on the attack. How is the response to asking the police to stop using violence more police violence? Every day there are more examples of such footage. It becomes too much, too much. Polls show the increase in the population who approve of the Black Lives Matters protests, even compared to what those same poll numbers might have been but three months earlier. They rage and they protest, and begin to offer something new: hope, against what might have been hopeless.

Aoife's preschool speaks of reopening. We'd already decided she wouldn't return. The provincial guidelines speak of reopening daycares and child care facilities starting June 12, although her preschool is in the midst of renovations to the point that next week would be impossible. We want our girls to interact with other children, but also aren't in any hurry to have them leave the house again. Ever, it would seem.

Over the past few weeks, becoming more aware of just how much we sit in the midst of history: the protests and subsequent conversations around race and police response, and just how much power we have to help shape where we go next. Police departments around the United States respond in a variety of ways. Some pull back, some lash out. Some officers are fired, some leave their jobs. Toronto's police chief unexpectedly announces that he, too, will step down. If the history of the origins of the police in the United States, according to John Oliver, was to keep the Black population in line, first as slaves and then as "free men," one has to also look north, at the Royal Canadian Mounted

Police, originally set up to keep the Aboriginal population in line. Look north, then. Look north and look west.

To say: we are still on lockdown. To say: we are nervous about the idea of schools reopening in September. I know a number of parents who are. How will the children keep six feet apart? they ask. I don't know. I just don't know. And how might they emerge? Might our off-spring be more hesitant to reach out, or more willing to jump? Will our wee two become far closer through this process, and might the only child become more distant? Or closer to their parents? What might the differences be? What might be the effects? I am writing to you from the inside, wondering how the picture looks. The picture, from here, is far from complete.

It rains. It rained yesterday, as well. The fires rage in Alabama, Milwaukee. The rages rage.

•

I'm at roughly 140 letters composed and mailed out since the lockdown began, and remarkably few people have written back. Why do so few write back? My original logic was to reach out to those in isolation, to potentially allow a variety of far-flung friends to feel less isolated. And yet my project, also, is a way to counter my own isolations, reaching out. Why do so few reach back? I write a letter, I write a letter, I write a letter. While I did not begin this project with the thought of expectation, per se, only six mailed responses in return is far less than I might have hoped for. And what of my isolation?

On the National Public Radio site, Los Angeles journalist and writer Elise Hu offers in her May 24 article, "What I Learned from Writing Letters to Strangers Across America":

> These days, we're stripped to our most primal longings to survive. And survival for humans means connection and communion wherever we can find it. It might be especially crucial for my generation. A quarter of millennials said in a YouGov survey last year that they have no acquaintances; 27% reported having no close friends and 30% said they had no best friends. And that was before the crisis hit.

Should I have been spending my days writing *her* letters, instead? Her short article ends:

> So many of the feelings my pen pals shared with me mirrored my own. I wrote to them originally to process my fears and anxieties during this time. In the end, the respondents helped me remember the clarifying thing about this pandemic—that we're all part of one community of humans. For the duration

of this crucible, and beyond, we should celebrate that which makes us most human: perspective, surprise and connection. Letters to strangers—and from strangers—can satisfy all three.

Christine works in the garden, and requests the young ladies assist by collecting small containers of topsoil from the withering bag in our driveway. It gives them a task, after all. The bag is less than half full, so they find it easier to shovel out dirt from the inside. This is how I discover them: Aoife standing inside the bag of topsoil with her shovel, and Rose just beside her, holding the blue recycling bin to collect it. Tonight, they will both require baths.

Bloomsday. The BBC reports that the "low-dose steroid treatment dexamethasone" has been proven "a major breakthrough in the fight against" the Covid-19 virus, able to "cut the risk of death by a third for patients on ventilators. For those on oxygen, it cut deaths by a fifth." This is progress, finally.

Twelve years ago, sitting this day in an Irish pub on Bloor Street West in Toronto, having drinks and conversation with poets Andy Weaver and Marcus McCann. Unthinkable, now. Both in that possibility and in that distance.

I am reading through Susan Howe's latest, her *Concordance*, attempting to reach the centre:

> As a relic of the typewriter generation, my field is the page with its harmonics—something to do with breath and keys that puncture. I know brilliant alluring virtuosities both strange and terrible are inevitable. Faster better technologies—deep space, non-real reality—"O brave new world that has [no paper] in it."

Lately, upon waking, I find sticky spots on the kitchen floor. Rose has discovered where the honey is kept, and daily, upon waking, prepares herself honey toast. I set to wiping the honey, once more, from the surfaces. We used to keep the toaster on a high shelf in the pantry, and the honey on a high shelf in the cupboards, but leave both out now, given Rose is clearly climbing to retrieve them. I would rather leave them both out and accessible than have her fall. I appreciate her fearlessness, but I shouldn't be testing that.

NASCAR bans the Confederate flag. That's good, but isn't it a bit late? Weren't the *Dukes of Hazzard* reruns quietly removed from broadcast a few years back for similar reasons? Statues of Confederate generals are pulled down, and American military officials speak of American army bases named for those on the Confederate side to potentially be renamed, which, of course, President Trump is completely against. So much of this moves in the right direction, although with the confusion that these ideas weren't considered far earlier. What country names bases after the leaders of an army that fought against their own? Why were there Confederate statues in Washington, DC, at all? It's more baffling than anything else.

As with some statues pulled down a few years ago, falling easily because they were cheaply made. A nineteenth-century plan to get statues up.

●

For a few weeks now, Christine has been talking of setting up our sunroom as her daily workspace, unable to continue working from the master bedroom. If these shutdowns are to continue long-term, there must be new ways for her to actually work. Today, also, I read Eliza Gabbert's essay in the "Pandemic Files" series over at the *Yale Review*, where she writes of adapting to this "new normal":

> Over the course of the first month, I read for longer and longer stretches, as though building my strength back up after an injury. When I couldn't read and wasn't working or sleeping, I chain-smoked crosswords, a kind of verbal solitaire that made a decent substitute for human conversation. One night I read for hours (*Rebecca* by Daphne Du Maurier—it helped that it was both suspenseful and a little silly) without looking at my phone. By mid-April, I felt that my reading comprehension and concentration were back to normal. I spent an afternoon with a new book of poetry and made notes for a review—a peaceful reprieve. When I called my best friend, who lives in Brooklyn with her husband and toddler, she too was feeling better; she'd reached a plane of acceptance. We'd developed new routines; we had to admit we were lucky. Same feelings, same order. It's as if our interior lives that once felt so variegated, so individual, were just the result of having slightly different experiences at different times.

Our young ladies take it upon themselves to start cleaning. They argue that they should start on the dishes, which would involve me supervising Rose teaching Aoife to handwash. I am at my desk. I'm not against the idea, but I convince them that sorting and putting away their laundry is more pressing. Eventually Aoife begins to Swiffer the kitchen floors, and Rose has three laundry bins upended through our bedroom, their bedroom, and the adjoining hallway, seeking hangers to put away their mound of dresses. They are hard at work, both of them. Aoife completes her work on the floors and returns to help Rose put away laundry. Their clothes lay scattered, but I can already see progress.

Christine is in the sunroom, in the midst of a work call. I sent her an email as a heads-up, in case she wanders through the chaos.

It is reported that Vera Lynn, World War II singer and "Forces' sweetheart" has died, at the age of 103.

One hundred days. June 22, 2020. The first one hundred days are, tra-ditionally, the first test of American presidents, what they accomplish. How the rest of their tenure might be shaped. What shape have we become? I have my own work to do, still. The Aunt Jemima brand is pulled and retired, as PepsiCo finally acknowledges that the brand and image were based on racial stereotypes. Confederate statues all across the United States are pulled down. A sign for Penny Lane in Liverpool is defaced. Despite the fame that came through the Beatles, the street is most likely named after eighteenth-century Liverpool industrialist and slave trader James Penny. In 1916, anti-German sentiment caused a vote for the town of Berlin, Ontario, to change its name to Kitchener, named after British general Horatio Herbert Kitchener, 1st Earl Kitch-ener, who had recently died. Given Kitchener's "scorched earth" impe-rial campaigns in Africa and India, the debate to rename begins once again, away from any association with the late general. This feels like the beginning of a long road, but one that moves in the right direction.

•

On June 24, a CBC.ca headline: "Experts Warn Parts of U.S. on Verge of Being Overwhelmed by COVID-19 Resurgence." As multiple states ignore warnings and have been reopening over the past few weeks, they wipe out two months' worth of progress on Covid-19 response.

While new cases have been declining steadily in early U.S. hotspots such as New York and New Jersey, several other states set single-day case records this week, including Arizona, California, Mississippi, Nevada, Texas and Oklahoma. Some of them also broke hospitalization records, as did North Carolina and South Carolina.

"People got complacent," said Dr. Marc Boom, CEO of the Houston Methodist hospital system. "And it's coming back and biting us, quite frankly."

Wilmington, North Carolina: three police officers are fired for comments they made as part of a video, looking forward to the upcoming "race war." One said he was ready to shoot as many Black people as possible, aiming to wipe them off the face of the earth. Tell me again we don't have a problem with racism?

My eldest daughter, Kate, has returned to work, but is wary of public transit. Her grandmother wants her car back. A few weeks ago, OC Transpo announced that wearing a mask was mandatory for bus service in the city. I was surprised it had taken so long. On the back of our front door, Christine maintains an array of face masks and coverings, once they are newly washed. They can be worn only once, before placed once more in the wash. She keeps a fresh one in our car as backup, although she was forced to remove the hand sanitizer she'd kept there. Apparently the onset of late spring into summer meant the car would heat up too much, suggesting a danger in an alcohol solution set under the pressure of extreme heat. What could go wrong?

July 1: our young ladies wish to sit with their chairs on the front lawn, facing the sunset. Rose wishes to watch as it lowers. In the absence of official fireworks this year, Christine allows it, letting them stay up later than they normally would. They sit with their lawn chairs some eight to ten feet apart, facing west, into the street.

The end of lockdown. The end of pandemic. Might it be, returning to Neil Gaiman's *The Sandman*, the feeling of waking up, back in the world? Perhaps wiser, perhaps more aware of how we need to adapt. Stretching our limbs and wiping our eyes and stepping back out, toward each other and into the world. We are not yet there.

Acknowledgments

Some of these pieces, often in earlier drafts, have appeared on the author's blog, Patreon patron-only blog, and Patreon page, as well as online at *Empty Mirror*. The poem on page 60 is from *The Book of Frank*. Copyright 2010 by CAConrad. Used with permission of the author and Wave Books.

Thanks to those friends who were kind enough to offer feedback and encouragement on earlier drafts, including Stephen Brockwell, Susanne Dyckman, Stephen Collis, Pattie McCarthy, b stephen harding, Lisa Fishman, and Julie Carr. Thanks to Stuart Ross for editorial feedback, and a final read.

This book is for those who came with me.

March 24–July 3, 2020
2423 Alta Vista Drive, Ottawa

It is easy to be beautiful; it is difficult to appear so. I admire you, beloved, for the trap you've set. It's like a final chapter no one reads because the plot is over.

—Frank O'Hara, "Meditations in an Emergency"

Born in Ottawa, Canada's glorious capital city, rob mclennan currently lives in Ottawa, where he is home full-time with the two wee girls he shares with Christine McNair. The author of more than thirty trade books of poetry, fiction and non-fiction, he won the John Newlove Poetry Award in 2010, the Council for the Arts in Ottawa Mid-Career Award in 2014, and was longlisted for the CBC Poetry Prize in 2012 and 2017. In March, 2016, he was inducted into the VERSe Ottawa Hall of Honour. His most recent poetry titles include *A halt, which is empty* (Mansfield Press, 2019), *Life sentence,* (Spuyten Duyvil, 2019) and *the book of smaller* (University of Calgary Press, 2022). In spring 2020, he won 'best pandemic beard' from Coach House Books via Twitter, of which he is extremely proud (and mentions constantly). He spent the 2007-8 academic year in Edmonton as writer-in-residence at the University of Alberta, and regularly posts reviews, essays, interviews and other notices at robmclennan.blogspot.com